I0420976

Arthur Asa Berger

Critical Modalities

Six Theorists on Communication, Culture and Society; Media Criticism; Humor; The Semiotics of Blonde Hair; Advertising; Gender; Tourism and Consumer Culture

Marin Arts Press

ISBN—13: 978-1517053246

ISBN—10: 1517053242

Contents

Acknowledgments

Most of the material in the book has never been published. The first chapter, "Six Theorists" was written when the editor of my book *50 Ways to Understand Communication* asked me to do a second edition. I wrote some new chapters for the book and then she decided she didn't want to do a new edition because she was more interested in having me do a fifth edition of my book on advertising for her. So I decided to use it in this book.

The second chapter, "Media Criticism" was written in English and translated into Chinese for a Chinese book on media and I'm using it with the permission of the publisher. A version of the third chapter, "A Rabbi, a Priest and an Imam Get a Haircut" was written for a Chinese Journal of Semiotics. I sent a first draft of an article and the editor asked me to write a more substantial version. I wrote the longer version—twice as long as the original—only to discover that, by mistake, the journal published the shorter version.

The chapter "Was Medusa a Blonde: On the Semiotics of Hair Coloring" I wrote because I was interested in the subject and thought I might eventually publish it in a semiotics journal. The chapter titled "In the Labyrinth" was given as a conference on visual semiotics in Argentina, which I had the pleasure to attend when I was a Fulbright Senior Specialist there and spent a month lecturing at various places on my work on media, popular culture and semiotics. This is followed by a review-essay of Benjamin DeMott's book *Supergrow: Essays and Reports on Imagination in America.* The review was written to be used as the introduction to a new printing of the book, but professor DeMott eventually decided to write his own introduction. The last chapter, "Tourists as Consumers, Consumers as Tourists," was written while I was a visiting professor at the Hong Kong Polytechnic University School of Hotel and Tourism Management. There is some redundancy in the book, but it is minimal.

I want to think all the editors and conference conveners who asked me to write something for them, and the book and journal editors who gave me permission to use my material. I did all the drawings and took the photographs found in the book—other than the photographs found in advertisements.

Six Theorists on Communication, Culture and Society

In this discussion, I offer a quotation of interest from an important communication theorist and then I discuss the passage. What this essay does is offer an important st atement by the theorists, so you can see the styles in which they write and get an insight into their thinking. I deal with:

1.   Jean Baudrillard on advertising and simulations

2.   Harold Garfinkel on ethnomethodology and everyday life

3.   Clothair Rapaille on imprinting and culture codes

4.   Henri Lefebvre on terrorism and everyday life

5.   Wolfgang Iser on the role of the reader

6.   Judith Butler on the social construction of gender

Jean Baudrillard

1. Advertising and Simulations

Any analysis of the system of objects must ultimately imply an analysis of discourse about objects—that is to say, an analysis of promotional "messages" (comprising image and discourse). For advertising is not simply an adjunct to the system of objects; it cannot be detached there from, nor can it be restricted to its "proper" function (there is no such thing as advertising strictly confined to the supplying of information). This lack of proportion is the "functional" apotheosis of the system. Advertising in its entirety contributes a useless and unnecessary universe. It is pure connotation. It contributes nothing to production or to the direct practical application of things, yet it plays an integral part in the system of objects not merely because it relates to consumption but also because it itself becomes an object to be consumed. A clear distinction must be drawn in connection with advertising's dual status as a discourse on the object and as an object in its own right. It is a useless, unnecessary discourse that it comes to be consumable as a cultural object....Advertising sets itself the task of supplying information about particular products and promoting their sale. In principle this "objective" function is still its fundamental purpose. The supplying of information has nevertheless given way to persuasion— even to what Vance Packard calls "hidden persuasion," the aim of which is a completely managed consumption....Studies have shown, however, that advertising's persuasive power is not as great as had been supposed. A saturation point is soon reached: competing messages tend to cancel each other out and many claims fail to convince on account of their sheer excessiveness. Moreover, injunctions and exhortations give rise to all kinds of counter-motivations and resistances, whether rational or irrational.

Jean Baudrillard, *The System of Objects*. London: Verso.   1996 164-165.

Jean Baudrillard (1929-2007) was an influential French sociologist who made important contributions to social and cultural theory. His book, *The System of Objects,* was published in France in 1968 and then was translated by James Benedict and published in English in 1996. It was based on his doctoral dissertation. Baudrillard was interested in consumer culture and in the impact of postmodernism on society. He suggested that in postmodern societies, like the one found in the United States, simulations become dominant and are more important that what they copy. In hyperreality, the sign becomes more important than what it stands for.

Thus, he explains in a celebrated article, "The Precision of Simulacra" in *Simulacra and Simulation,* Disney   and is the "real" America and the real America is an imitation of Disneyland. He writes:

> Everywhere in Disneyland the objective profile of America, down to the morphology of individuals and of the crowds, is drawn. All its values are exalted by the miniature and the comic strip....Disneyland exists in order to hide that it is the "real" country, all of the real America that is Disneyland....Disneyland is presented at imaginary in order to make us believe that the rest is real, whereas all of Los Angeles and the America that surrounds it are no longer real but belong to the hyperreal order and to the order of simulation. (European Graduate School, n.d.)

In Baudrillard's "hyperreality" view of America, it is becoming more and more like Disneyland. As Peter Brooker explains in his book *Cultural Theory: A Glossary* (1999: 121-122):

> **Hyperreality.** A term associated with the effects of MASS PRODUCTION and REPRODUCTION and suggesting that an object, event, experience so reproduced replaces or is preferred to its original: that the copy is "more real than real." In the writings of the French social philosopher and commentator on POSTMODERNISM, Jean Baudrillard (1929--) and Umberto Eco (1932--), hyperreality is associated especially with cultural tendencies and a prevailing sensibility in contemporary American society.
>
> In Baudrillard's discussion, hyperreality is synonymous with the most developed form of SIMULATION: the autonomous simulacra which is free from all reference to the real.

Baudrillard and many other European cultural theorists have focused their attention on the role of simulations and the hyperreal in America, and have been fascinated—perhaps even obsessed—with Disneyland and what it reflects about contemporary American culture and society.

Harold Garfinkel

2. Ethnomethodology and Everyday Life

From the point of view of sociological theory the moral order consists of rule governed activities of daily life. A society's members encounter and know the moral order as perceivedly normal courses of action—familiar scenes of everyday affairs, the world of daily life known in common with others and with others taken for granted. They refer to this world as the "natural facts of life" which, for members, are through and through moral facts of life. For members not only are matters so about familiar scenes, but they are so because it is morally right or wrong that they are so. Familiar scenes of everyday activities, treated by members as the "natural facts of life," are massive facts of the members' daily existence both in the real world and as the product of activities in the real world....In every discipline, humanistic or scientific, the familiar common sense world of everyday life is a matter of abiding interest. In the social sciences, and in sociology particularly, it is a matter of essential preoccupation....Despite the topic's centrality, an immense literature contains little date and few methods with which the essential features of socially recognized "familiar scenes" may be detected and related to dimensions of social organization. Although sociologists take socially structures scenes of everyday life as a point of departure they rarely see, as a task of sociological inquiry in its own right, the general question of how and why any such common sense world is possible....Procedurally it is my preference to start with familiar scenes and ask what can be done to make trouble....I have found that they produce reflections through which the strangeness of an obstinately familiar world can be detected. (pages 35,36, 37)

Harold Garfinkel, *Studies in Ethnomethodology.* Englewood Cliffs, NJ: Prentice-Hall. 1967

Harold Garfinkel (1917 to 2011) taught sociology for many years at the University of California at Los Angeles and was one the founders and most important exponents of the branch of sociology known as ethnomethodology. Ethnomethodologists are interested in what people do in everyday life and the common understandings they have that make it possible for people to get along with another, live together in families, and the way people make sense of the world. We don't think very much about what we take for granted, but it is the common understandings we have, as reflected in our conversations and routine behaviors, that make the world go around.

In one experiment, Garfinkel asked his students to insist that people clarify commonplace remarks. In one case someone said to one of Garfinkel's students, "I had a flat tire." The student-experimenter then said "What do you mean when you said you had a flat tire?" The person who had the flat tire was stunned for a moment and replied "What do you mean what do you mean?" Garfinkel's point was that many of our everyday interactions are based on the assumption that when someone says "I had a flat tire," the person hearing that statement will understand what was meant. In his book he cites a number of experiments when his students asked for clarifications for simple statements that led to exasperation and sometimes anger on the part of the persons making these statements.

In another experiment, he asked students to pretend that they were boarders (that is, strangers) for fifteen minutes to an hour in their homes. They were meant to make all descriptions "behaviorally," which meant they were to write an account of the experience acting as if they didn't know any history or background of the members of their families and didn't concern themselves with motives. Thus, one student wrote "A short, stout man entered the house" to describe her father, and she did the same for everyone in her family. Many of Garfinkel's students said they were unable to sustain this perspective because there was so much bickering and arguing and manifestations of hostility among members of the family.

Garfinkel devised another experiment in which students pretended they were boarders in their homes and thus were excessively polite, avoided getting personal with their family members and only spoke when spoken to. The students conducting this experiment reported that their families were "stupefied," and many were upset with the behavior of the students, even after the students explained their behavior was an assignment in one of their classes. They asked questions like "what's got into you?" or "were you fired?" or "did you break up with your girlfriend?" That was because the students didn't take larger portions of food than they should have, didn't interrupt other members of the family when they were talking, didn't bicker with others, and so on.

Generating situations that have people question the organization of familiar scenes and engender "accounts" and "explanations" for their occurrence was a method Garfinkel used to make v isible the "seen-but-unnoticed," i.e. the taken for granted organization of situations. In later studies, he moved on from using "breaching experiments" to observe the fine detailed organization of the production and design of actions through which people make accountable, that is "observable-and-reportable," the organization of situations.

What Garfinkel and other ethnomethodologists teach us is that our everyday activities are much more interesting and complex than they seem, at first glance. There is point in examining the finest details of people's actions because they embody our knowledge, competence and reasoning. Ethnomethodologists, we may say, are sociologists who take second glances.

Clotaire Rapaille

3. Imprinting Codes

Most of us imprint the meanings of the things most central to our lives by the age of seven. This is because emotion is the central force for children under the age of seven....An imprint and its Code are like a lock and its combination. If you have all the right numbers in the right sequence, you can open the lock. Doing so over a vast array of imprints has profound implications. It brings to us the answer to one of our most fundamental questions: why do we act the way we do? Understanding the Culture Code provides us with a remarkable new tool—a new set of glasses, if you will, with which to view ourselves and our behaviors. It changes the way we see everything around us. What's more, it confirms what we have always suspected is t rue—that, despite our common humanity, people around the world really *are* different. The Culture Code offers a way to understand how. Once an imprint occurs, it strongly conditions our thought processes and shapes our future actions. Each imprint helps make us who we are. The combination of imprints defines us....Even our most arbitrary actions are the result of trips we take down our mental highways. We take these trips hundreds of time a day, making decisions about what to wear, what to eat, where to go, what to say in conversation, and so on. What most people do not realize, however, is that there is a Code required to make these journeys. Think of a Code as a combination that unlocks a door. In this case, we need not only to punch in the numbers, but also to punch them in in a specific order, at a specific speed, with a specific rhythm, etc.

Clotaire Rapaille, *The Culture Code: An Ingenious Way to Understand Why People Around the World Live and Buy as They Do.* Broadway Books, NY. Pages: 11, 21, 24.

Clotaire Rapaille, a French psychoanalyst and marketing expert, argues that countries are all different because of the way children are socialized and "imprinted" from their birth to the age of seven. In essence, what happens is that children learn certain codes about food, clothing, manners, and all kinds of others as they grow up and these "imprints" shape their behavior, in large measure, for the rest of their lives. What we call culture, in the anthropological sense, can be thought of as the pattern of codes people learn when they grow up in different culture and subcultures. These different codes explain why French people are so different from English people who are so different from American people who are so different from Mexican people who are so different from Chinese people who are so different from Japanese people...and on and on it goes. Some people are able to change their codes—if for the example, they emigrate from China to the United States, especially if they move when they are young.

Rapaille offers an extreme example which involves the way French people and American people think about cheese. The French code for cheese is "alive," and so they do not refrigerate it but keep it in containers (cloches) where is ages and starts to smell. The American codes for cheese is "dead," and so they kill the cheese through pasteurization, wrap it in plastic and put it in what he calls "morgues," that is—refrigerators. American cheese is often pre-wrapped, what he calls "mummified" and then kept in refrigerators. If you go to fancy food shops, you now find cheese, from many good cheese-making countries, that is not pre-wrapped—but most Americans still probably keep that cheese in their refrigerators.

He discusses any number of other topics that show the differences between people in different countries and explains these differences by the imprinting that children undergo as they grow up. By seven, Rapaille argues, they have become Americans, Italians, Chinese, whatever and probably will remain so for the rest of their lives. As a result of travel, people become exposed to other cultures and often take good things (French cheese, champagne) and bad things (McDonald's hamburgers) from the countries they visit. This does not mean we are becoming a monoculture—in which we are all the same; it means our tastes have broadened and are more eclectic. So the codes can be modified but not changed to any substantial degree.

HENRY LEFEBVRE

4. Terrorism and Everyday Life

Any society involving, on the one hand, poverty and want and on the other a privileged class (possessing and administering, exploiting, organizing and obtaining for its own ends as much social overtime as possible, either for ostentatious consumption or for accumulation, or indeed for both purposes as once) is maintained by the dual method of (ideological) *persuasion* and *compulsion* (punishment, laws and codes, courts, violence kept in store to prevent violence, overt violence, armed forces, police, etc.) A class society (and we know as yet no other) is a repressive society....A *terrorist society* is the logical and structural outcome of an *over-repressive* society; compulsion and the illusion of freedom converge; unacknowledged compulsion besiege the lives of communities (and of their individual members) and organize them according to a general strategy....In a terrorist society terror is diffuse, violence is always latent, pressure is exerted from all sides on its members who can only avoid it and shift its weight by a super-human effort; each member is a terrorist because he wants to be in power (if only briefly); thus there is no need for a dictator; each member betrays and chastises himself; terror cannot be located, for it comes from everywhere and from every specific thing; the "system" (in so far as it can be called a "system") has a hold on every member separately and submits every member to the whole, that is, to a strategy, a hidden end, objectives unknown to all but those in power, and that no one questions.

Henri Lefebvre, *Everyday Life in the Modern World.* 1971. New York: Harper and Row. Pages 143, 144, 147. Translated by Sacha Rabinovich.

On the cover of Henri Lefebvre's (1901-1991) classic *Everyday Life in the Modern World,* we see a table with a checkered tablecloth on which this is a bottle of milk, a glass of milk, and a bowl of cereal in front of a window. In the window we see an atom bomb exploding. This cover deals with the topic of the book—the ordinary nature of everyday life and the extraordinary nature of class societies where, according to Lefebvre, we all live in terrorist societies and our lives are shaped by unacknowledged compulsions. Lefebvre was a Marxist who used various aspects of everyday life to make his argument about, as he saw things, the destructive nature of capitalist societies.

He believes that everyday life, not economics, was the sphere where class based societies were dominated by elites and suggested that we can counter the repressive nature of these societies by making our everyday lives become a "work of art," and encouraging the rediscovery of "festival."   In the Middle Ages, festivals were the means by which peasants escaped—for a limited period of time--the drudgery of their daily lives and the repressive nature of the Catholic church.   Lefebvre was an extremely influential professor who taught at a number of French universities and whose work fell in and out of favor many times during the case of his long life.

Wolfgang Iser

5. The Role of the Reader

...In considering a literary work, one must take into account not only the actual text but also, and in equal measure, the actions involved in reacting to that text....The text as such offers different "schematized views" through which the subject matter of the work can come to light....If this is so, then the literary work has two poles, which we might call the artistic, and the aesthetic: the artistic refers to the text created by the author, and the aesthetic to the realization accomplished by the reader. From this polarity it follows that the literary work cannot be completely identical with the text, or with the realization of the text, but in fact must lie halfway between the two. The work is more than the text, for the text only takes on life when it is realized and furthermore the realization is by no means independent of the individual disposition of the reader--though this in turn is acted upon by the different patterns of the text. The convergence of text and reader brings the literary work into existence, and this convergence can never be precisely pinpointed, but must always remain virtual, as it is not to be identified either with the reality of the text or with the individual disposition of the reader....A literary text must therefore be conceived in such a way that it will engage the reader's imagination in the task of working things out for himself, for reading is only a pleasure when it is active and creative. In this process of creativity, the text may either go not far enough or may go too far, we may say that boredom and overstrain form the boundaries beyond which the reader will leave the field of play.

Wolfgang Iser. "The Reading Process: A Phenomenological Approach." In David Lodge, ed. *Modern Criticism and Theory: A Reader.* New York: Longman. 1988. (pages 212, 213)

Wolfgang Iser (1926-2007) was one of the proponents of "reception theory," which marked a shift from focusing on texts themselves, and their structure and techniques of composition, to the audiences of texts and the role they play in the scheme of things. Reception theorists suggests that all texts have "gaps" or "lapses" in them which enables different readers to read the same texts differently and find different meanings in them. We are not talking about taste here—there's no disputing taste, and Iser's focus is not on whether you like a text or not, but on the indeterminate nature of texts, of the way they can have so many meanings to different people, based on their education, socio-economic class, cultural sophistication and so on.

Terry Eagleton's *Literary Theory: An Introduction* (Minneapolis: University of Minnesota Press, 1983: 74) explains the relationship that exists between reception theory and other approaches to literature—a by extension, mass mediated culture, pop culture…whatever you want to call what we see on television, when we go to see films and so on. He writes:

> Reception the4ory examines the reader's role in literature, and as such is a fairly novel development. Indeed one might very roughly periodize the history of modern literary theory in three stages: a preoccupation with the author (Romanticism and the nineteenth century); an exclusive concern with the text (New Criticism); and a market shift of attention to the reader over recent years. The reader has always been the most underprivileged of this trio—strangely, since without him or her there would be no literary texts at all. Literary texts do not exist on bookshelves: they are processes of signification materialized only in the practice of reading. For literature to happen, the reader is quite as vital as the author.

Eagleton wrote his book in 1983 and since his book was written new approaches to literature have happened such as the rediscovery, so to speak, of semiotic theory and the influence of postmodernism, post-colonial theory and Feminism on contemporary thought.

Judith Butler

6. Is Gender Socially Constructed?

Is there "a" gender which people are said to *have* or is it an essential attribute that a person is said to *be*, as implied in the question "What gender are you?" When feminist theorists claim that gender is the cultural interpretation of sex or that gender is culturally constructed, what is the manner or mechanism of this construction? If gender is constructed, could it be constructed differently, or does its construction imply some form of social determinism, foreclosing the possibility of agency and transformation? Does "construction" suggest that certain laws generate gender differences along universal axes of sexual differences? How and where does the construction of gender take place? What sense can we make of a construction that does not assume a human constructor prior to that construction? On some accounts, the notion that gender is constructed suggests a certain determinism of gender meanings inscribed on anatomically differentiated bodies, where those bodies are understood as passive recipients of an inexorable cultural law. When the relevant "culture" that "constructs" gender is understood in terms of such a law or set of laws, then it seems that gender is as determined and fixed as it was under the biology-is-destiny formulation. In such a case, not biology but culture, becomes destiny.   On the other hand, Simone de Beauvoir suggests in *The Second Sex* that "one is not born a woman, but, rather, becomes one." For Beauvoir, gender is "constructed," but implied in her formulation is an agent, a *cogito,* who somehow takes on or appropriates that gender and could, in principle, take on some other gender....There is nothing in her account that guarantees that the "one" who becomes a woman is necessarily female.

Judith Butler, *Gender Trouble: Feminism and the Subversion of Identity.* New York: Routledge.

The material quoted from Judith Butler's book, *Gender Trouble,* comes from a section titled "Gender: the Circular Ruins of Contemporary Debate" in which she suggests there are problems with many of the formulations writers have made that gender is "social constructed."   She points out that saying gender is "social constructed" often only means it is as determined as the biology-is-destiny formulations, except that it is culture that is the determinant, not biology.   Her book is generally thought to be one of the key texts in Feminist theory.   It is not, let me point out, an easy book to read and her argument is carried on at a very high level of intellectual sophistication.

David Gauntlett, a British media and cultural theorist, discusses Butler's work as follows and offers the following insights into her work:

> Butler argues that we all put on a gender performance, whether traditional or not, anyway, and so it is not a question of whether to *do* a gender performance, but what form that performance will take. By choosing to be different about it, we might work to change gender norms and the binary understanding of masculinity and femininity. This idea of identity as free-floating, as not connected to an 'essence', but instead a performance, is one of the key ideas in queer theory. Seen in this way, our identities, gendered and otherwise, do not express some authentic inner "core" self but are the dramatic *effect* (rather than the cause) of our performances.

> http://www.theory.org.uk/ctr-butl.htm

This notion, that gender is a performance, suggests that we look upon gender differently than we've done in the past.   Gender is not something we are born with but something that we adopt, for one reason or another, to suit our purposes.   Her thinking about gender also involves a rejection of binary oppositions as the way to make sense of gender.   Binary thinking works as follows: if male, not female and if female, not male.   But if gender is a performance, binary oppositions no longer matter.

Media Criticism

Let me begin by offering my understanding of the terms I'll be using in this discussion of media criticism. A *medium*, technically speaking, is a means of facilitating communication between two or more people. When we talk to a friend, we are using the medium of speech to communicate our ideas. In the past fifty years or so, with the development of new technologies of mass communications, we now think about "media" differently. We use it to deal with communication between a small number of people, who create and perform the texts carried by the mass media, and large numbers of people—the audiences—who receive the mass mediated communication. With the development of the Internet, things have changed considerably and now individuals can communicate with large numbers of people through blogs and comments on social media such as Facebook or Twitter. It is possible for someone to have hundreds or even thousands or hundreds of thousands of "friends" who receive their messages on blogs, tweets on Twitter and postings on Facebook.

The second term, *criticism,* originally involved evaluations of literary texts but has now evolved, when tied to media, to mean the analysis of the social, economic, psychoanalytic, political, aesthetic and cultural significance of various kinds of communication—and, more specifically, mass mediated communication, sometimes called mass-mediated culture. Usually this criticism involves the applications of theories that help critics make their analyses. In the realm of film studies, for example, there are both books on film theory and books that apply these theories by film critics. Critics, we may say, always have some theories that shape their analyses. In some cases, critics apply theories from a number of disciplines or subject areas and this has led to a new meta-discipline, cultural studies. My focus in this paper is on some of the more important theories that inform media criticism and various aspects and kinds of texts that have to be taken into consideration when doing media criticism. Below I offer a timeline for the development of media, which shows when the most important technologies of media were created.

Timeline for Development of Media

1833	Mass Circulation Newspapers
1876	Telephone
1926	First Radio Network
1927	First Sound Film
1933	FM Radio
1962	First Communications Satellite
1969	Internet
1972	First Video Game: Pong
1975	Personal Computer
1978	Cellular Phone Service
1981	Music Television
1991	World Wide Web
1995	Digital Cell Phones
1996	Google
2001	MP3 Technology
2002	Satellite, Web-Based Radio and Television
2004	Facebook
2006	Twitter

2007   Apple iPhone introduced.

2010   Apple iPad introduced.

2011   Sixteen billion indexed Web pages on Internet

2012   Google Glass, wearable computers become popular.

2012   Advanced Smart Watches.

2014   Occulus Virtual Reality Headphone

2014   Right to be forgotten" ruling in Europe

2015   Apple Smart Watch

Media Usage in the United States

We can see from this timeline that the development of new technologies and modifications of older media technologies in recent years have played an important role in our daily lives and, in particular, in shaping our time use. The average person in the United States, as the statistics below indicate, watches more than four hours of television, listens to the radio for more than one and a half hours and spends around an hour on cell phones every day. Other countries may show similar statistics on media usage. Media criticism is important because people spend so much time with the media and its texts. The statistics on media usage in the United States are quite remarkable, averaging almost twelve hours per day in 2015..

Average Time Spent per Day with Major Media by US Adults, 2011-2015
hrs:mins and CAGR

	2011	2012	2013	2014	2015	CAGR (2011-2015)
Digital	3:40	4:20	4:51	5:15	5:38	11.4%
—Desktop/laptop*	2:33	2:27	2:19	2:22	2:22	-1.8%
—Mobile (nonvoice)	0:48	1:35	2:16	2:34	2:51	37.2%
—Other connected devices	0:18	0:18	0:17	0:19	0:25	7.8%
TV**	4:34	4:38	4:31	4:22	4:15	-1.8%
Radio**	1:34	1:32	1:30	1:28	1:27	-2.0%
Print**	0:44	0:38	0:32	0:26	0:21	-17.0%
—Magazines	0:18	0:16	0:14	0:12	0:10	-13.5%
—Newspapers	0:26	0:22	0:18	0:14	0:11	-19.8%
Other**	0:39	0:38	0:31	0:26	0:24	-11.7%
Total	11:11	11:46	11:55	11:57	12:04	1.9%

Note: ages 18+; time spent with each medium includes all time spent with that medium, regardless of multitasking; for example, 1 hour of multitasking on desktop/laptop while watching TV is counted as 1 hour for TV and 1 hour for desktop/laptop; *includes all internet activities on desktop and laptop computers; **excludes digital
Source: eMarketer, April 2015

188127   www.eMarketer.com

Average Time Spent Per Day with Major Media by U.S. Adults

Let me offer some statistics now on the media usage of young people, taken from research conducted by the Kaiser Family Foundation on "Media Use Over Time Among all 8- to 18-year-olds."

> Five years ago, we reported that young people spent an average of nearly 6½ hours (6:21) a day with media—and managed to pack more than 8½ hours (8:33) worth of media content into that time by multitasking. At that point it seemed that young people's lives were filled to the bursting point with media. Today, however, those levels of use have been shattered.
>
> Over the past five years, young people have increased the amount of time they spend consuming media by an hour

and seventeen minutes daily, from 6:21 to 7:38—almost the amount of time most adults spend at work each day, except that young people use media seven days a week instead of five.

Moreover, given the amount of time they spend using more than one medium at a time, today's youth pack a total of 10 hours and 45 minutes worth of media content into those daily 7½ hours—an increase of almost 2¼ hours of media exposure per day over the past five years.

http://www.kff.org/entmedia/upload/8010.pdf

If young people and adults spend that much time each day with the media, the questions naturally arises—what effects does all this involvement with the media have on us as individuals and on society?

There is a debate among media critics about the impact of the mass media upon individuals and society. Some critics suggest the media now bring us the arts and information that refine us culturally and enhance our understanding of politics and other aspects of society. They argue, also, that our exposure to the violence that permeates the mass media is not harmful because it acts as a catharsis. Thus, the effect of exposure to media violence does not lead individuals to become violent but diffuses their anger and purges them of it. We can call them "catharsis" critics. The term originated in the writings of Aristotle. Those on the opposite side of the fence argue that the impact of media is much more powerful and longer lasting than the "catharsis" critics believe and while social scientists haven't been able to prove that there's a connection between exposure to violence and violent behavior, there is often a correlation that should make us be concerned. There is a kind of contagion effect in which some disturbed individuals, who are exposed to violence on television and in films, are led to imitate it. Thus, in the United States, in recent years there have been a series of mass murders—the most terrible being the killing of twenty school children and six adults by a disturbed twenty-year old man on December 14, 2012. This followed shortly after another mass killing a while earlier in the United States.

Focal Points in the Study of Media

There are, I suggest, four focal points we can consider in dealing with the media. First, we have the medium itself and each medium imposes certain restrictions on the texts they carry and offer various possibilities as well. The most important medium for most people all over the world is television. As the figures above show, many Americans watch four hours of television each day. Next, we can consider the texts, or in the case of television, the programs it carries. I will call them "Art works." Works of art are created by writers and directors and performers. I will call them "Artists." The programs and other texts carried by television are consumed by "Audiences," of varying natures. Finally, the "Audiences" are parts of a larger entity, namely society. In the United States, I call this entity "America." The diagram below shows the relationships that exist among the focal points. There are arrows pointing in both directions among all of the focal points, which suggests that each of them affects and is affected by one or more of the other focal points.

This chart is a modification of one made by M.H. Abrams, a literary theorist, in his book *The Mirror and the Lamp*. Abrams differentiated between works that were *mirrors* and reflected society and works that were *lamps*, and projected a writer's (or any kind of creative artist) view of things on society. He also discusses *pragmatic* theories of art that claim art is important because it can be used to do things (like sell products) and *emotive* theories of art that deal with how works of art can generate strong feelings in audiences. These four theories of art are shown below:

Pragmatic   A tool, does something, is functional

Objective   A record, projects artist view of society

Emotive   Generates Emotions in audiences

Mimetic   Mirrors society (from Aristotle's theory

of mimesis)

In his chart, Abrams had four items: the Universe, Work, Artist and Audience. He didn't have a medium because he was talking about works of literature in print and so the medium didn't play an important part in his concerns. My chart includes media because it plays a central role in our considerations and because there are many different media that might be part of our investigations such as print, television, radio, video and photography. Imagine eight lines with arrows pointing in both directions between all items].

Art   Artist

            Medium

Audience   America

One can investigate the relation that exists between an artist and a medium, between an artist and society, between a work of art or text and an artist, between a work of art and a medium, between a work of art and society, and so on. There are numerous possibilities. In addition, critics can deal with three focal points or ever four focal points. Marshall McLuhan, in his book *Understanding Media,* focuses his attention on the media, per se, though in other works, such as *The Mechanical Bride,* he is concerned about what genres of art, like advertisements and comic strips, reveal about American culture and society.

Critics who focus on creators and their texts tend to do biographical research. Critics who focus on the impact of texts on audiences or on America (or any society) tend to do sociological research. Many critics focus their attention on texts, the medium that carries them, and their impact on audiences and society, at large. Media criticism, as I understand the term, deal with one or more of these focal points and is not confined to a particular medium, such as television or film or video games.

McLuhan made a distinction between what he called "hot" media, which have a great deal of information and "cool" media, which have little information.

As he writes in *Understanding Media* (1965:22-23):

There is a basic principle that distinguishes a hot medium like radio from a cool one like the telephone, or a hot medium like the movie from a cool one like TV. A hot medium is one that extends one single sense in "high definition." High definition is the state of being filled with data. A photograph is, visually, "high definition." A cartoon is "low definition," simply because very little visual information is provided. Telephone is a cool medium, or one of low definition, because the ear is given a meager amount of   information...Hot media are, therefore, low in participation, and cool media are high in participation or completion by the audience.

His ideas are shown in the table that I have made, taken from his discussion of the topic in the second chapter of *Understanding Media.*

Hot Media	Cool Media
High definition (full of data)	Low definition (little data)
Low participation (excludes)	High participation (includes)
Movie	Television program
Radio	Telephone
Photograph	Cartoon
Printed word	Speech
Lecture	Seminar
City	Small town

McLuhan suggests that medium is more important than the texts or messages the medium carries because, as he wrote in *Understanding Media* (1965:18), "the effects of technology do not occur at the level of opinions or concepts, but alter sense rations or patterns of perception steadily and without resistance." That is why he was able to proclaim, enigmatically, "the medium is the message." The most important thing for McLuhan was the way media shapes our perceptions. In this respect, he discusses print media, which are linear (we read lines of type) and this, he suggests, encourages rationality, uniformity, continuity, individualism and nationalism. He contrasts print with electronic media, which are inclusive and immediate. McLuhan fell into disfavor among many academics for a number of years but with the development of social media, his ideas about "global villages" now resonate and he has become increasingly popular.

Aristotle, the First Media Critic

It was Aristotle who gave us many of the important insights that we now use in criticizing and interpreting mass mediated texts. He was writing about poetry and the theater, but his approach is worth considering. His *Poetics,* written around 330 B.C., was one of the most influential analyses of literature   and communication ever written and shaped the thinking of critics, literary theorists, and rhetoricians for more than a thousand years. He argues that literary works should be seen as imitations of reality and that there are three matters we must consider relative to imitation—the medium of imitation, the objects imitated and the mode of imitation. This theory is known as *the mimetic theory of art,* which I dealt with in my discussion of the ideas of M.H. Abrams..

Aristotle discusses the difference between the arts that rely on words alone in contrast to those that employ a number of different media. For example, we can think of the difference between a novel and a film made from that novel. Then he discusses the objects of imitation and writes:

> Since the objects of imitation are men in action, and these men must be either of a higher or a lower type (for moral character mainly answers to these divisions, goodness and badness being the distinguishing marks of moral difference), it then follows that we must represent men either as better than in real life, or as worse, or as they are. (Aristotle, 1941, in Smith, J.H. & Parks, E.W. (eds.) *The Great Critics: An Anthology of Literary Criticism,* 1951, p. 30)

Aristotle later describes "men in action" as the way to define plot. He then differentiates between comedy and tragedy, writing that comedy is "an imitation of persons inferior—not, however, in the full sense of the word bad, the Ludicrous being merely a subdivision of the ugly. It consists of some defect or ugliness which is not painful or destructive." (p.33). He contrasts comedy with tragedy which, he explains, "is an imitation of action that is serious, complete, and of a certain magnitude."

This leads him to discuss how tragedy should be presented. He offers some suggestions about how tragedy should be performed and writes (p. 34) "Now as tragic imitation implies persons acting, it necessarily follows, in the first place, that Spectacular equipment will be part of Tragedy. Next, Song and Dance, for these are the media of imitation." Aristotle is presenting some of the more important elements of narrative which involves plot, character and even production values. Plot, the arrangement of the incidents in texts and character, the qualities that agents have, are the basic considerations. He also distinguishes between simple plots, that involve changes of fortune without reversals or recognitions and complex plots that have reversals, recognitions or both.

Narrative theory is important because we must recognize that a large percentage of television programs are narratives. As Martin Esslin writes in *The Age of Television* (1982:7):

> On the most obvious level television is a dramatic medium simply because a large proportion of the material it transmits is in the form of traditional drama mimetically represented by actors and employing plot, dialogue, character, gesture, costume--the whole panoply of dramatic means of expression....According to the 1980 edition of *The Media Book*, in the Spring of 1989 American men on average watched television for over 21 hours per week, while the average American woman's viewing time reached just over 25 hours per week. The time devoted by the average American adult male to watching dramatic material on television thus amounts to over 12 hours per week, while the average American woman sees almost 16 hours of drama on television each week. That means the average American adult sees the equivalent of *five to six full-length stage plays a week!*

We have to recognize that the most diligent theater-goer doesn't even see one play a week. In addition, many texts that are not dramas or fictions still have a narrative structure, so narratives play an important role in most mass mediated texts. Aristotle provided insights into narratives but also, with his discussion of the difference between comedy and tragedy, ideas about another important topic related to media criticism—genres.

Genres

Genres are kinds of texts and when people decide to go to see a film or to watch a television program, it is usually because it is a genre they like: mysteries, science fiction, romance, news, sports and so on. In his essay "Television Images, Codes and Messages," the critic Douglas Kellner discusses genres and their role in our mass-mediated culture:

> A genre consists of a coded set of formulas and conventions which indicate a culturally accepted way or organizing material into distinct patterns. Once established, genres dictate the basic conditions of cultural production and reception. For example, crime dramas invariably have a violent crime, a search for its perpetrators, and often a chase, fight, or bloody elimination of the criminal, communicating the message "crime does not pay." The audience comes to expect these predictable pleasures and a crime drama "code" develops, enshrined in production and studio texts and practices. (*Televisions*, 7, 4, 1974)

These conventions, he explains, make is easy for audiences to anticipate and to understand what happens in a text and make it easier for writers to create these texts. That is because they can assume certain expectations on the part of audiences and use formulas, with minor variations, to satisfy these expectations. If one were to distinguish between conventional texts, like classical detective mysteries (think of Sherlock Holmes or Hercule Poirot) and Avant Garde texts full of invention (think of James Joyce's *Ulysses*), genres would be classified as highly conventional texts. *Ulysses,* we must recognize, is an important example of intertextuality—being based on Homer's *The Odyssey.*

Now, I will relate these genres to the uses and gratifications approach to media criticism, which focuses not on the alleged effects of media and mass mediated texts on individuals and societies but on the way members of audiences use specific texts and genres and the gratifications they derive from them. Genres, we must remember, come and go. At one time there were more than thirty westerns broadcast on American television networks and now there are hardly any. Romance novels are extremely popular now and so are science fiction and spy stories and films. Also, new genres are continually being invented, such as talent shows (singing shows and dancing shows) that are part of what is known as "reality television."

Some of the earliest research in this area was described as follows by Katz, Blumler and Gurevich (1979:215):

> Herzog (1942) on quiz programs and the gratifications derived from listening to soap operas; Suchman (1942) on the motives for getting interested in serious music on radio; Wolfe and Fiske (1949) on the development of children's interest in comics…Each of these investigations came up with a list of functions served either by some specific contents or some medium in question: to match one's wits against others, to get information or advice for daily living, to provide a framework for one's day, to prepare oneself cultural   for the demands of upward mobility, or to be reassured about the dignity and usefulness of one's role.

Uses and gratifications research is problematic for some media critics because it doesn't lend itself to quantification and because critics can disagree about how to apply the approach to events in texts and determine which gratifications a given event in a text confers on members of audiences. I offer, now, a chart with some of the more important uses and gratifications and my suggestions about which genres provide these gratifications.

Uses and Gratifications	Genres
To satisfy curiosity and be informed	Documentaries, News Shows, Talk Shows, Quiz Shows
To be amused	Situation Comedies, Comedy Shows
To identify with the deity and divine	Religious Shows
To reinforce belief in justice	Police Shows, Law Shows

To reinforce belief in romantic love	Romance novels, Soap operas
To participate vicariously in history	Media Events, Sports Shows
To see villains in action	Police Shows, Action-Adventure Shows
To obtain outlets for sexual drives in a guilt free context	Pornography, Fashion Shows, Soft Core Commercials, Soap Operas
To experience the ugly	Horror shows
To find models to imitate	Talk Shows, Action Shows, Award Shows, Sports Shows, Commercials
To experience the beautiful	Travel Shows, Art Shows, Culture Shows (Symphony Concerts, Operas, Ballet)

We can see that genres play an important role in the decision making of individuals about what kinds of texts and in the genres they want to consume—in media such as books, comic books, television, films, and video games. Most works of popular culture, in whatever medium, are genre works that are looked down upon by many critics as being produced for the "lowest common denominator." These texts are part of the "culture of the masses" as contrasted to elite cultural texts that are part of the "culture of the classes" (classes here being cultural elites). Postmodernists, as I shall explain shortly, do not consider works of elite culture and popular culture to be different in any important ways.

Levels of Media Theory and Criticism

I will now jump a couple of thousand years from Aristotle to the contemporary scene and discuss some of the more important critical approaches to the media, and, in particular, to texts carried by the media. I will do this by suggesting that there are three levels of media theory and criticism. At the highest level, we have the theorists who have shaped much of the modern debate about media. I refer here to seminal thinkers such as:

Level A: Seminal Thinkers

Aristotle, Karl Marx (and other Marxist thinkers), Sigmund Freud, Carl Jung, Ferdinand de Saussure, Charles S. Peirce, Mikhail Bakhtin, Emile Durkheim, Claude Lévi-Strauss, Marshall McLuhan and Vladimir Propp.

At the level below them, at level B, are thinkers who applied and often moved beyond the theories of the seminal thinkers, but who are extremely important thinkers in their own right. I refer to theorists who have applied, often brilliantly, the ideas of the seminal thinkers and in many cases added new ideas:

Level B: Giants: Important Thinkers Who Have Applied Ideas of Seminal Thinkers

Roland Barthes, Umberto Eco, Stuart Hall (and his colleagues at the University of Birmingham),   Jean Baudrillard, Michel de Certeau, Antonio Gramsci, Bruno Bettelheim and Theodor Adorno   (and   the   Frankfurt School).

Below them are:

Level C: All other media critics.

That is, all the contemporary media critics and scholars who have been influenced by the seminal theorists and often by the "giants" at level B, as well.

Roland Barthes

Our extremely important media critics are generally influenced by the seminal theorists.

For example, in the preface to the 1970 edition of *Mythologies,* Roland Barthes writes (1972:9):

> This book has a double theoretical framework: on the one hand, an ideological critique bearing on the language of so-called mass culture; on the other, a first attempt to analyze semiologically the mechanics of this language. I had just read Saussure and as a result acquired the conviction that by treating "collective representations" as sign-systems, one might hope to go further than the pious show of unmasking them and account in detail for the mystification which transforms petit-bourgeois culture into a universal nature.

In this quotation, Barthes mentions Ferdinand de Saussure and alludes to Karl Marx and, by mentioning "collective representations," the great French sociologist, Emile Durkheim. Barthes' *Mythologies* has, in turn, been enormously influential and has turned the attention of many media scholars to advertising, wrestling (which Barthes explains is really theater), material culture, and popular culture in general.

France, Germany and Russia have produced a disproportionate number of the most important media theorists and culture critics. Since the media have only been with us for approximately the past hundred years, it is logical that most of the more important media theorists and critics are contemporaneous and did their work in the past hundred years. Some of these thinkers didn't write about mass media but their ideas have been useful to media critics.

Below I list the more important disciplines used by media critics. We must recognize that many media critics use a number of these disciplines at the same time. Also, it is difficult to know where to place a theory. Does narrative theory belong under semiotics or literary theory? The quotation from Roland Barthes, at the beginning of his *Mythologies,* is an example of the way critics often combine disciplines, as in the meta-discipline cultural studies.

Semiotics.

Semiotics is defined as the science of signs and semiotic critics use the theories of Ferdinand de   Saussure and Charles S. Peirce, the founders of the science, in their work. There have been many   developments   in semiotics over the years and it plays an important role in cultural studies, a topic   that I will discuss shortly. Among the most important contemporary media critics using semiotics   are Yuri Lotman, who founded the Tartu school of semiotics and the Italian scholar Umberto Eco.

Semioticians are interested in what signs are, how they work, and, in their writings, they apply concepts such as metaphor,   metonymy,   denotation,   connotation, postmodernism and intertextuality.   Semiotics I would suggest is the core discipline of cultural studies.

Psychoanalytic Theory.

It was Freud whose many books described psychoanalytic theory and many media critics apply   insights   from Freud and Jung in their work. Basic to psychoanalytic theory are concepts such   as the unconscious, the Oedipus complex, defense mechanisms, dreams and sexuality. One of the   most interesting psychoanalytic theorists is Bruno Bettelheim, who uses psychoanalytic theory in   his analysis of fairy tales, *The Uses of Enchantment*. Jung's book *Man and His Symbols* is a   useful guide to his theories and how they can be applied. The work of the folklorist Alan Dundes   is informed by psychoanalytic theory.

Marxist/Ideological Theory.

Marx remains an influential theorist for media critics, even though his economic theories are no   longer considered   important.   Marx   and   other   important ideological theorists wrote about topics such as alienation, class conflict, materialism, the relation between the base and the superstructure and what we now call consumer cultures. We may say that Marxist theory informs   the work of the   Italian theorist, Gramsci, the Frankfurt

School and of the Birmingham school of cultural studies.

Sociological Theories

Theories by sociologists such as Georg Simmel and Emile Durkheim, and many contemporary   sociologists, are often used by media critics. They apply concepts such as anomie, functionalism, stereotyping, content analysis, uses and gratifications and mass society in their investigations.

Leo Lowenthal's article on biographies in popular American magazines, published in 1944, is an example of content analysis and critical theory. He discovered that before World War I, most of the biographies were of politicians and businessmen and celebrated production. After World War I, the biographies were of entertainers, movie stars, and celebrities and celebrated consumption.

Other important sociologically informed media critics are Elihu Katz and Herbert Gans.

Aesthetic Theory

For our purposes, media aesthetics deals with the way those who create mass mediated texts achieve the effects they want—by the use of camera, color, editing techniques, and music to generate the effects they want on audiences. Sergei Eisenstein's books *Film Sense* and *Film   Form* are important examples of aesthetic criticism. In *Film Form,* Eisenstein's develops his   concept of montage—a concept that has influences film makers to this day. The development of what is called "Visual Culture" makes use of aesthetic theory.

Anthropological Theory

The central concept in anthropology is "culture" and while most anthropologists do not deal directly with the mass media, their ideas are often used by critics. The work of the French anthropologist Claude Lévi-Strauss has been applied by media critics—especially Lévi-Strauss's work on myths and structuralism. His analysis of the Oedipus myth provides media critics with a methodology that they can apply to mass mediated texts.

Literary Theory

Earlier I discussed the work of M.H. Abrams, who was an important literary theorist. Literary theory investigates the devices writers use to achieve their effects. There is a vast literature, starting with Aristotle, that deals with questions of interest to literary theorists.   Many critics have a background in literary theory and use concepts they find in the works of contemporary theorists in various fields. Literary theorists are interested in matters such as the nature of narratives, in genres, and in reception theory, also known as reader response theory—which argues that readers play an important role in bringing texts to life and what readers know shapes their perceptions of works. Vladimir Propp's *The Morphology of the Folktale,* first published in 1928, is a seminal analysis of narratives.

Feminist Theory.

In recent years, Feminist scholars have developed a body of writings that focus upon gender and the way women have been portrayed in mediated texts of all kinds. There have been two waves of Feminist critics but the main focus in both waves is upon the way women are oppressed in societies and this is reflected in the media in these societies which they characterize as patriarchal and phallocentric. If you look at the roles women play in many narrative texts you find that they are exploited for their bodies and sexuality and the media, in general, support sexual inequities. Some important Feminist studies are: Susan Gubar, *The Madwoman in the Attic: The Woman Writer and the Nineteenth-Century Literary Imagination*; and Toril Moi. *Sexual/Textual Politics: Feminist Literary Theory.*

Queer Theory

Judith Butler's *Gender Theory* is one of central texts in Queer Theory. The term "queer" was a slang term commonly used by heterosexuals to describe lesbian women and gay men and others   in the Lesbian, Gay, Bisexual and Transgender community. The LGBT has appropriated the term and use it now for their own purposes. Queer theory argues that gender is socially constructed and is not all based on nature. The quote below characterizes queer theory:

> Gender studies and queer theory explore issues of sexuality, power, and marginalized populations (woman as other) in literature and culture. Much of the work in gender studies and queer theory, while influenced by feminist criticism, emerges from post-structural interest in fragmented, de-centered knowledge building (Nietzsche, Derrida, Foucault), language (the breakdown of sign-signifier), and psychoanalysis (Lacan).

http://owl.english.purdue.edu/owl/resource/722/12/

We can see how Queer Theory combines many different approaches, in its attempt to counter the discrimination it finds in phallocentric societies and the texts produced in these societies.

****

There is a wonderful scene in *Casablanca* in which Humphrey Bogart has just shot a German officer. Claude Rains, who is the police chief, then says to an associate "Round up the usual suspects." That is what I think, to myself, when there is a text I want to criticize. "Which combination of the techniques of analysis will offer the most interesting analysis?" Often this involves using different methodologies for different parts of aspects of a given text.

Problems Faced by Media Critics: Applying Concepts Correctly

One problem we face in criticizing a mass mediated text (and I consider criticism, analysis, and interpretation to be the same thing, for all practical purposes) involves how good a job we do in using the concepts at our disposal and how complete our analysis is. If we neglect important parts of a text, for one reason or another, we may not be giving a text the kind of analysis it deserves. And if we do not apply a concept correctly, our analysis will be suspect. There is also the matter of using as many techniques as are appropriate, so that we cover all the important aspects of a text.

Yuri Lotman, a semiotician from Tartu, Estonia, has written in his book, *The Structure of the Artistic Text* (1977:17) "The tendency to interpret *everything* in an artistic text as meaningful is so great that we might rightfully consider nothing accidental in a work of art."   Shortly after this, he explains why this is the case. He writes (1977:23):

> Since it can concentrate a tremendous amount of information into the "area" of a very small text (c.f. the length of a short story by Cexov and a psychology textbook), an artistic text manifests yet another feature: it transmits different information to different readers in proportion to each one's comprehension: it provides the reader with a language in which each successive portion of information may be assimilated with repeated reading. It behaves as a kind of living organism which has a feedback channel to the reader and thereby instructs him.

So we learn two important things from Lotman: first, everything in a text is meaningful and nothing is accidental and second, the more you know, the more you can find in a text. Because artistic texts are so rich, we can reread them or see them again and each time we get more out of them and find different things in them.

Let me apply Lotman's theories to an imaginary advertisement with a man and two women in it. We can ask the following questions (this draws on my discussion of this topic in my book *Ads, Fads and Consumer Culture*) and is a kind of primer for those interested in visual images and visual culture:

I will begin with an imaginary print advertisement in which we find a photograph of a man and two women and some written material. Here's a list of possible topics to consider in analyzing the advertisement.

1.   What is the graphic design of the advertisement?   Do we find axial balance or an asymmetrical relationship among the elements in the advertisement?   Why is the design important?

2.   How much copy is there relative to the amount of pictorial matter? Is this relationship significant in any respect?

3.   Is there a great deal of blank (white) space in the advertisement or is it full of graphic and textual material? Generally speaking, the more white space you have in an advertisement, the more upscale the product being advertised is.

4.   What angle is the photograph shot at? Do we look up at the people in the advertisement? Do we look down at them from a height? Or   do we look at them from a shoulder-level position? What significance does the angle of the shot   have? Are they looking at us? If so, what does that mean?

5.   How is the photograph lit? Is there a great deal of light or is there a little light and very dark shadows (chiaroscuro lighting)? What is the mood found in the advertisement and generated by it? Why was that mood used?

6.   If the photograph is in color, what colors dominate? What significance do these colors have?

7.   How would you describe the three figures in the advertisement? Consider such matters as facial expression, hair color, hair length, hair styling, fashions (clothes, shoes, eyeglasses design and jewelry), various props (a cane, an umbrella),   body shape, body language, age, gender, race, ethnicity, signs of occupation, signs of educational level, relationships suggested between the male and females, objects in the background, and so on.

8.   What is happening in the advertisement? What does the "action" in the photo suggest? Assume that we are seeing

one moment in an ongoing narrative. What is this narrative and what does it reveal about the three figures?

9.   Are there any signs or symbols in the photograph? If so, what role do they play?

10.   In the textual material, how is language used? What arguments are made or implied about the people in the photograph and about the product being advertised? That is, what rhetorical devices are used to attract readers and stimulate desire in them for the product or service? Does the advertisement use associations or analogies or something else to make its point?

11.   What typefaces are used in the textual parts of the advertisement? What importance do the various typefaces have? (Why these typefaces and not other ones?)

12.   What are the basic "themes" in the advertisement? How do these themes relate to the story implied by the advertisement and the product or service being sold?

13.   What product or service is being advertised? Who is the target audience for this product or service? What role does this product or service play in American culture and society?

14.   What values and beliefs are reflected in the advertisement? Sexual jealousy? Patriotism? Motherly love? Brotherhood of man? Success? Power? Good taste?

15.   Is there any background information you need to make sense of the advertisement? How does context shape our understanding of the advertisement?

16.   Does the advertisement have a "unique selling point?" If , what is it?

17.   If the advertisement has a logo, what is it like? What would a semiotician make of the logo?

This list of questions does not cover every aspect of an advertisement but it does direct our attention to various aspects of advertisements that might be considered when interpreting a typical print advertisement found in a newspaper or magazine. You can see that advertisements can be extremely complex texts, even if many fashion ads show little but models and corporate logos and have almost no text.

Problems Media Critics Face: A Pedagogic Note on Theory and Practice

I had the pleasure of giving a series of lectures in Argentina in 2012 and spent a good deal of time with a number of professors there and they all complained about the same thing. They told me that while they could teach their students theories or methodologies such as semiotics, and the students could learn these methodologies and pass tests on them, the students didn't have the slightest idea of how to apply semiotics to anything. One reason for this is that theory is intoxicating and the professors enjoyed teaching semiotic theory, for example, but didn't give any thought to teaching their students how to apply semiotics to texts or anything else. And they didn't know how to do so. In other words, the professors created many students who knew a lot of semiotic theory but didn't know what they could do with semiotics. That is a problem I faced many years ago and I spent a number of years developing learning games and activities which required my students to apply the concepts they learned to specific texts.

My answer to the professors was "less theory and more practice." I played a learning game with one group of professors in which they dealt with the metaphor "a department store is a cathedral." I broke them into groups of three and had them see in which ways department stores were like cathedrals and they had a wonderful time playing the game. I explained to the professors that they had to develop a number of learning games and exercises to help the students learn to apply the theories they learned. I believe that it is extremely important that students not only learn theories involved in media criticism but learn how to apply these theories. And that is why my articles and books generally have two parts to them: one that deal with theories and another that applies these theories.

Problems Faced by Media Critics: Reading Things into Texts

There is a problem we face in analyzing media texts called "the God's truth versus the Hocus Pocus" dilemma. "God's truth" means the critics are finding things in the texts or bodies of texts that are in them but which may not be evident. "Hocus Pocus" means that what critics find in texts are not in the texts but in their minds and read into them.

For example, some critics are adept at finding mythic themes in narrative texts: films, television shows, and novels. The questions we must ask are: Is this mythic material actually in the text? Did the creators of these texts consciously insert this material or, possibly, unconsciously insert it? Does what the creators of texts intend mean anything? Critics who find intertextual connections between texts are often accused of reading these connections into the texts, which raises a question: how do media critics prove that their analyses are correct or, even more to the point, can they ever do so?

Let's consider Vladimir Propp's classic *Morphology of the Folktale* in this respect. Propp studied a collection of a certain kind of Russian folktales and found structural components in them which he elaborated in his book. He developed his typology, he explains, because none of the other means of dealing with folktales, such as dealing with themes or plots or motifs or classifying them one way or another, were adequate. As Propp explains (1928/1968:6), "fairy tales possess a quite particular structure which is immediately felt and which determines their category, *even though we may not be aware of it*." [My italics.] He then lists an initial situation and thirty-one functions of dramatis personae that, he argues, informs fairy tales—from the first, absentation (in which one of the members of a family absents himself from home) to the last (the hero is married and ascends the throne).

Propp's morphology is important because his list of functions can be applied to many modern texts, such as James Bond novels and films and just about any narrative. As Alan Dundes writes, in his "Introduction to the Second Edition" of Propp's book (1968:xiv):

> Cultural patterns normally manifest themselves in a variety of cultural material. Propp's analysis should be useful in analyzing

the structure of literary forms (such as novels and plays), comic strips, motion picture and television plots, and the like. In understanding the interrelationship between folklore and literature, and between folklore and the mass media, the emphasis has hitherto been principally on content. Propp's *Morphology* suggests that there can be structural borrowings as well as content borrowings.

I should point out that Propp's breakthrough involved examining a collection of texts in the same genre. Looking at one of his folktales wouldn't have enabled him to find the structure he discovered in his collection of tales.

Propp's book is a contribution to the *syntagmatic* analysis of media texts. A syntagm is a chain and a narrative can be seen as a chain or sequence of events. The other important way of analyzing texts is based on Lévi-Strauss's work and is called *paradigmatic* analysis. It looks for a set of polar oppositions in a text that generate meaning. Saussure had written (1915/1966) "In language there are only differences." This approach is based on the notion that meaning is based on relationships and that the most important relationship in the production of meaning in language is the binary opposition. As Jonathan Culler explained in his book *Structuralist Poetics: Structuralism, Literature and the Study of Literature* (1976:15) "Structuralists have generally followed Jakobson and taken the binary opposition as a fundamental operation of the human mind basic to the production of meaning."

In theory, then, some interrelated binary oppositions exist in all texts and the task of the critic is to find these oppositions. One problem is that different media critics often find different sets of binary oppositions. This raises the question of whether the sets of oppositions that media critics find in texts are in the texts or in the minds of the critics. Let me offer an example of the way critics can disagree with one another when making paradigmatic analyses of texts. The distinguished Italian semiotician, Umberto Eco analyzed Ian Fleming's *Dr. No* and suggests that the basic opposition in *Dr. No* is between James Bond and Dr. No, with Honeychile Rider, the heroine, functioning as a mediating figure. I would argue that there is a different set of opposition that, I believe, explains the book and various relationships better. In my analysis of the book I see Dr. No and Honeychile Rider as opposites, with James Bond playing a mediating role. Let me offer the opposition I find in the book:

Honeychile Rider	Bond	Dr. Julius No
Beautiful		Ugly
Natural		Mechanical
White		Yellow
Female		Male
Victim		Villain
Lives		Dies
Males Love to Bond		Is Killed by Bond

My argument is that these oppositions are the dominant ones in the book: male/female, beautiful/ugly, white/yellow and so on. It is James Bond who mediates between Honeychile and Dr. No and resolves the opposition by killing him. The question we might ask is—who is right when critics come up with different paradigmatic analyses of texts? I would answer this by suggesting that the critic whose oppositions explains the book better is the correct one.

New Directions in Media Criticism: Cell Phone Use

In Vincent Miller's "New Media, Networking and Phatic Culture" that appeared in *Convergence: The International Journal of Research Into New Media,* he writes (2008):

> Through a consideration of the new media objects of blogs, social networking profiles, and microblogs, along with their associated practices, I will argue that the social contexts of "individualization" and "network sociality," alongside the technological developments associated with pervasive communication and "connected presence," has led to an online media culture increasingly dominated by phatic communications. That is, communications which have purely social (networking) and not informational or dialogic intents. I conclude with a discussion of the potential nihilistic consequences of such a culture.

Phatic communication is, in essence, noises people make, such as "uh huh," "yeah," that indicate they are attentive but don't have much content. If many teenagers send, on average, one hundred messages a day with their cell phones (and this usually takes around ninety minutes), they can't communicate much content, so it is reasonable to suggest that most of these messages are phatic in nature. A considerable amount of the ninety minutes that teens spend using their cell phones is devoted to texting—and now, for a small percentage of teens, a new wrinkle, sexting, in which they send semi-nude and sometimes nude images of themselves to their friends and other people. Of course, once an image is sent to someone by cell phone, it can be forwarded on to other people or even uploaded to Facebook or YouTube, where millions of people can see it.

New Directions in Media Criticism: Social Media

Young people are consuming something like 34 gigabytes of data each day from around five hours a day of watching screens of one kind or another: computer monitors, cell phone screens, video game player screens, and television screens. In an article by Nick Bilton (2009), in the *New York Times,* he discusses a study by researchers at the University of California in San Diego that found that the average American reads or hears something like 100,000 words a day from the Web, the radio, television, and other media and that consumption of media has increased around 350% in the last 30 years. Thus, while we read less print media we spend a good deal of time reading from screens during a typical day. It is estimated that many Americans spend more than eight hours a day watching screens of one kind or another: mostly on cell phones, computer monitors, and televisions sets.

From a sociological perspective, we have all kinds of demographic data on users of media in the United States and other countries. We can break the users down along national, racial, gender, socioeconomic, age, and other kinds of classifications. And we know, for example, that the use of media has increased over the past ten years in most groups. The question we can't answer with any certainty is, What effects does all this media usage have upon us as individuals and upon the societies in which we live? Let's consider the users of Facebook, the most important social medium of recent years. It now has more than a billion people who use it and seems to be growing every month. The figures below provide an idea of where Facebook is most popular as of 2014.

Users (Millions)	Country
151	USA
108	India
70	Brazil
60	Indonesia
44	Mexico
30	United Kingdom
26	Japan
22	France
22	Germany
18	Italy

Source: Statistica. Numbers rounded by author.

As I understand the term *social media,* it refers to sites such as Facebook, Twitter, LinkedIn, and YouTube that enable people to send messages, images, and videos that can be read or seen by large numbers of people. We can access these social media sites on the Internet with our computers, tablets, and cell phones. In the passage that we find at the beginning of this chapter, Vincent Miller (2008) hypothesizes that much of the communication we do through social media is "phatic." These messages, sometimes called "small talk," as I explained earlier, do not communicate information as much as indicating we are present or we are paying attention. The huge numbers of texted messages young people send one another are caused more by the need to maintain their network of friends and consolidate their togetherness with one another than by the desire to convey information.

Media scholars used to describe the mass media as made up of a small number of "senders" (writers, actors, directors, filmmakers, and so on) who created texts and transmitted them through traditional mass media such as print, radio, and television to "receivers," that is, the large numbers of people who formed the audience. With the development of social media, the old (creator) sender-receiver (audiences) model has been obliterated since millions of people now are the creators of texts of all kinds— whether texted and sexted messages, images, or videos—that they place on YouTube or Facebook or other social media sites. Anyone with a digital camera, a cell phone that takes video images, or a video camera is now a potential video-maker, and they can send their images of videos to sites like YouTube which provide people with the means of broadcasting their works. The fact that YouTube has millions of people accessing its videos every day, that people are sending billions of "tweets" a year, and that Facebook now has a billion members demands the attention of media and communication scholars. If the social media are that popular, they must be doing something important (providing important gratifications) for all the people who use them.

We might ask ourselves, why do people spend so much time with their computers and cell phones, surfing the Internet, texting one another and sending images and texts to social-media sites? One reason, I believe, is that these devices enable people to connect with others and to ameliorate the alienation, loneliness and sense of separation many people feel in contemporary postmodern societies. This is particularly the case with adolescents, who have powerful needs for affiliation, who suffer from anxiety about what they are to become, and who often feel alienated and estranged from their parents, other members of their families, and often society itself.

Erik Erikson

According to the psychoanalyst Erik H. Erikson (1963), all adolescents have to deal with the rapid growth of their bodies and the problem of identity and role confusion they suddenly face. As he explains in his book *Childhood and Society* (2nd ed., Revised and enlarged):

it is the inability to settle on an occupational identity which disturbs individual young people. To keep themselves together they temporarily overidentify, to the point of apparent complete loss of identity, with the heroes of cliques and crowds. This initiates the stage of "falling in love," which is by no means entirely, or even primarily, a sexual matter—except where the mores demand it. To a considerable extent adolescent love is an attempt to arrive at a definition of one's identity by projecting one's diffused ego image on another and by seeing it thus reflected and gradually clarified. This is why so much of young love is conversation. (p. 262)

Erikson published his book in 1963, well before the development of cell phones, but his comments about adolescent needs and the quest for identity ring true and still apply today. He offers additional insights into the significance of cell phones for our psyches in his theory about the crises we all face as we grow older. According to Erikson, human beings all face certain developmental crises at different stages of their lives. Below I present a list of his crises, in the form of the polar oppositions he uses, and offer hypotheses about the role cell phones play in each of these crises. This material on our developmental crises is taken from his chapter "The Eight Ages of Man" in his book *Childhood and Society.* I have not dealt with infancy, when the first two stages take place, because infants don't use cell phones.

Stage	Crisis	Cell Phone Functions
Childhood	Initiative/Guilt	Family Integration, Play
School	Industry/Inferiority	Schoolwork Skills
Adolescence	Identity/Role Confusion	Peer Group Bonding, Romance,
Young Adult	Intimacy/Isolation	Love, Career, Initiation
Adult	Generativity/Stagnation	Career, Community
Maturity	Ego Integrity/Despair	Contact, Community

According to Erikson, we all face these crises and must find a way to resolve them successfully as we move from infancy to old age. His discussion of the crises that adolescents face—Identity/Role Confusion—is particularly interesting. At this stage, Erikson explains, young people are disturbed by their inability to settle upon an occupation and "temporarily overidentify, to the point of an apparent complete loss of identity, with the heroes of cliques and crowds." (page 261): He makes an insightful analysis of "young love" in his book *Childhood and Society* (1963):

> To a considerable extent adolescent love is an attempt to arrive at a definition of one's identity by projecting one's diffused ego image on another and by seeing it thus reflected and gradually clarified. This is why so much of young love is conversation. (page 261).

Thus, the countless text messages young people send one another have a deeper and more significant meaning than we might imagine, for they can be seen, among other things, as attempts at self-definition.

Young girls who become fans of Madonna or Lady Gaga or cute guy vampire actors or whomever and young boys who idolize football and other sports stars or other kinds of heroic figures are, Erikson would say, going through a stage in which they are struggling to consolidate their identities and using their heroes and heroines as a means toward accomplishing this task.

But why texting rather than talking? One reason is that texting is more private and another is that it is less direct. If you talk on your cell phone where there are other people, they sometimes can hear what you are saying to the person to whom you are talking. In addition, texting enables people to send messages without needing to be concerned about where the recipients of these messages are or what they are doing. When you text a message, you don't face the problem of having to actually conduct a conversation. But the goal of texting is to have a *kind* of impersonal conversation, and conversation, Erikson has explained, plays a crucial role in the lives of adolescents.

We can say that the social media create artificial or virtual communities of people. Thus, we can get "friends" and "followers" on Facebook and Twitter. The same kind of thing applies to other sites. In addition, there are actual communities of people interested in art, travel, or whatever that one can join on various social media sites. As of now, I have more than two-hundred "friends" on Facebook—most of whom I don't know and never will meet. My son-in-law has seven thousand Facebook friends; some people have tens of thousands. I have an acquaintance who has 195,000 friends for her blog on humor. There are, it turns out, some people on Facebook and other sites who collect as many "friends" as they can get. But are these "friends" really friends? Obviously not. Getting large numbers of "friends" on Facebook is a form of collecting, analogous to people who collect stamps or fountain pens or anything else. And this collecting is driven by psychological needs people have to excel in some way or to have mastery over something.

Cell phones and the social media represent a major transformation in the way societies function. The ubiquity of cell phones and the popularity of the social media are signifiers of a new social order in which anyone and almost everyone can make their presence known, by sending messages, photos, and videos that potentially can be accessed by a large number of people. This has had the effect of breaking the monopoly on sending messages using the mass media that was held by traditional print and electronic media. The popularity of cell phones and social media can also be seen as a signifier of the loneliness, alienation, and sense of separation that modern societies generate. Our use of cell phones and social media represents "escape attempts" in which we try to achieve a kind of electronic togetherness or virtual community. What the long-term consequences of the new media on American society and societies everywhere will be, for the new media are now global in nature, is hard to say. Many media critics and theorists connect the new media to my last topic, postmodernism.

LYOTARD

New Directions in Media Criticism: Postmodernism

According to Jean-Francois Lyotard, postmodernism can be defined as involving "incredulity toward metanarratives." Metanarratives are the all-embracing philosophical systems that characterized modernist thinking. As Lyotard writes in his book *The Postmodern Condition: A Report on Knowledge* (1984xxiii,xxiv):

> The object of this study is the condition of knowledge in most highly developed societies. I have decided   to use the word *postmodern* to describe that condition. The word is in current use on the American   continent among sociologists and critics; it designates the state of our culture following the transformations which, since the end of the nineteenth century, have altered the game rules for science, literature, and the arts. The present study will place these transformations in the context of the crisis of narratives....Simplifying to the extreme, I define *postmodern* as incredulity toward metanarratives. .To the obsolescence of the metanarrative apparatus of legitimation corresponds, most notably, the crisis of metaphysical philosophy and of the university institution which in the past relied on it. (p. xxiv)

In postmodern societies, Lyotard asserts, there are competing narratives and many different ways of making sense of the world, which has led to what he describes as a crisis of legitimation. We don't know   what's right and what's wrong. In addition to our not knowing what to believe, many postmodern theorists argue that it doesn't make any difference what we believe. It is generally held that postmodernism became dominant in the 1960s when there was a cultural mutation and a major shift in beliefs and values.

There are many differences between postmodernism and modernism. If modernism differentiates between elite arts, such as opera and ballet, and popular culture, postmodernism tears down the barriers between them and revels joyfully in mass culture. Modernism involves a stance of "high seriousness" towards life whereas postmodernism involves an element of game playing and an ironic stance as well as a kind of playfulness. People in postmodernist societies people "play" with their identities and change them when they feel bored with their old ones. And postmodern societies, as Baudrillard suggests, are characterized by illusions and simulations. Reality, he suggests, has been replaced by *hyperreality,* a situation in which the sign is now more important than the signifier it stands for. As Peter Brooker explains in *Cultural Theory: A Glossary* (1999:121-122):

> **Hyperreality.** A term associated with the effects of MASS PRODUCTION and REPRODUCTION and suggesting that an object, event, experience so reproduced replaces or is preferred to its original: that the copy is "more real than real." In the writings of the French social philosopher and commentator on POSTMODERNISM, Jean Baudrillard (1929–) and Umberto Eco (1932–), hyperreality is associated especially with cultural tendencies and a prevailing sensibility in contemporary American society. In Baudrillard's discussion, hyperreality is synonymous with the most developed form of SIMULATION: the autonomous simulacra which is free from all reference to the real.

That explains why Baudrillard believes that simulations are now more important and more real for people than the reality they were designed to imitate. Indeed, Baudrillard has even suggested that Disneyland is now the ultimate reality and the United States is an imitation of it! As the power of the Disney media corporation grows—and it has recently purchased Marvel comics and its heroes and Star Wars and its heroes-- some theorists argue that it is now playing a dominating role in shaping our collective consciousness.

With this brief discussion of postmodernism (there are countless books on the subject) I conclude this report on media criticism. There are 303 million sites on Google on media criticism and 13,900,000 sites on mass media criticism. It is an enormous subject and one that is of central importance in understanding contemporary culture and society in every country and one that I have been working on for the past fifty years.

References

http://www.kff.org/entmedia/upload/8010.pdf

http://owl.english.purdue.edu/owl/resource/722/12/

Aristotle (1941) in Smith, J.H. & Parks, E.W. (eds.) *The Great Critics: An Anthology of Literary   Criticism.* New York: W.W. Norton

Abrams, M.H. (1958). *The Mirror and the Lamp: Romantic Theory and the Critical Condition.* New York: W.W. Norton

Barthes, R. (1972). *Mythologies. (*Trans. A. Lavers.*)* New York: Hill & Wang.

Berger, A. A. (2011)   *Ads, Fads and Consumer Culture.*   4th Edition. Lanham, MD: Rowman & Littlefield.

Brooker, P. (1999). *Cultural Theory: A Glossary.* London: Arnold.

Culler, J. (1975).   *Structuralist Poetics.*   Ithaca, New York: Cornell University Press.

Eisenstein, S. (1942) *The Film Sense.*   New York: Harcourt Brace Jovanovich.

Eisenstein, S. (1949). *Film Form.* New York: Harcourt Brace Jovanovich.

Erikson, E. H. (1963). *Childhood and Society.* Second Edition Revised and Enlarged. New York: W.W. Norton.

Esslin, M. (1982). *The Age of Television.* San Francisco, CA: W.H. Freeman.

Katz, E., Blumler, J, & Gurevitch,M. (1979). Utilization of mass communication by the individual. In G. Gumpert & R. Cathcart (Eds.) *Inter/Media.* New York: Oxford University Press.

Kellner, D. "Television Images, Codes and Messages," 1980. *Televisions* 7 (4)   1974

Lotman, Y. (1977). *The Structure of the Artistic Text.*   Ann Arbor: Michigan Slavic Contributions.

Lyotard, J-F. (1984). *The Postmodern Condition: A Report on Knowledge.* Minneapolis: University of   Minnesota Press.

McLuhan, M. (1951). *The Mechanical Bride.* Boston: Beacon.

McLuhan, M. (1965). *Understanding Media: The Extensions of Man.* New York: McGraw-Hill.

Miller, V. (2008). "New Media, Networking and Phatic Culture," *Convergence: The International Journal of Research into New Media.*

Propp, V. (1968). *Morphology of the Folktale.* (2nd Edition). Austin: University of Texas Press.

Note: This chapter draws upon my writings such as *Media Analysis Techniques* 5th Edition; *Cultural Criticism: A Primer of Key Concepts; Ads, Fads and Consumer Culture; Making Sense of Media, Media and Communication Research Methods* 3rd Edition; and various articles I've written on myth, narratives and genres.

A Priest, an Imam and a Rabbi Get a Haircut

A Semiotic Analysis of a Jewish Joke

One of the more important books in the semiotic canon is Vladimir Propp's *Morphology of the Folktale.* In this book, Propp offers us thirty one functions that describe actions by characters who play an important role in folktales. These functions help us understand how narrative texts work. Some typical functions are interdiction, violation, trickery, and the receipt of a magical agent. Propp chose to focus on functions of characters in folktales because other approaches, such as studying themes or kinds of heroes and heroines, didn't work. As he explains (1968:7) "if a division into categories is unsuccessful, the division according to theme leads to total chaos. We shall not even speak about the fact that such a complex, indefinite concept as 'theme' is either left completely undefined or is defined by every author in his own way."

His solution to the problem of dealing with his texts was to offer a morphology of his texts. As he explained (1968:19), "We shall separate the component parts of fairy tales by special methods; and then we shall make a comparison of tales according to their components. The result will be a morphology (i.e., a description of the tale according to its component parts and the relationships of these components to each other and to the whole)." He then described 31 functions of characters found in his folk tales. He defined a function as (1968:21) "An act of a character, defined from its point of view of its significance for the course of action." These functions, he added, are stable and their number is limited.

I had not read Propp's *Morphology of the Folktale* when I started doing my research into what I describe as the most important techniques of humor. But after I read Propp's book (I had already finished my research and found 45 techniques that are similar in nature to his functions),, I considered using as a title for one of my books on humor, *The Morphology of the Joketale.* I have been interested in humor for many years and have dealt with it in a scholarly way from my 1965 dissertation on a humorous comic strip, *Li'l Abner,* to my books such as *An Anatomy of Humor, The Genius of the Jewish Joke, Blind Men and Elephants,* and *The Art of Comedy Writing,* all of which appeared in the 1970s. In the seventies, I did some research on what it is that generates humor in texts and found 45 techniques that, I argue, inform all humor. My first article in which I dealt with these techniques was "Anatomy of a Joke," published in the *Journal of Communication* in the summer of 1976. I argue that these techniques are at work in all humorous texts to generate mirthful laughter. They tell is what makes us laugh which is different from why we laugh.

A review of my book, *The Art of Comedy Writing,* offers an insight into the power of my typology:

> For the work that I am presently doing involving humor in British, American, and Irish literature, Arthur Asa Berger has provided a very insightful and useful methodology for analyzing and creating humorous discourse in his *The Art of Comedy Writing.* For me, his model is as powerful as such other discourse models as "Script Model Grammar," by Raskin and others, "Conversational Implicatures," by Grice and others, "Conversational Analysis," by Tannen and others, "Genre and Archetype Theory," by Frye, White and others, "Signification Theory," by Henry Lewis Gates and others, "Dialogic Theory," by Bakhtin and others, various ethnographic and linguistic models by Schiffrin and others, or indeed any discourse model I have studied and/or used. Although Berger's model is flawed in many ways, and although it is presented in a glib fashion, it is nevertheless a powerful and rigorous model. Its power comes from its detail (45 techniques of devices) and its rigor comes from how this detail is spelled out (15 "Language" devices, 14 "Logic" devices, 13 "Identity" devices, and 3 "Action" devices.

> Don L.F. Nilsen, *International Journal of Humor Research* (12-1, 1999-96,97)

Nilsen ended his review by saying he intended to use the book in a course he was teaching, which suggests that not only did he think my typology was powerful, but that it would be useful to him and his students. My focus on what techniques make us laugh, on the techniques that generate humor, is different from the research of most humor scholars, writers, and philosophers, from Aristotle's time to the present, who deal with theories about why we laugh.

The Four Why Theories of Humor

There are four dominant "why" we laugh theories. The first argues that humor is based on a sense of *superiority.* Aristotle said humor is based on (McKeon, 1941:1459) "an imitation of men worse than average; worse, however, not as regards any sort of fault, but only as regards one particular kind, the Ridiculous, which is a species of the Ugly. The Ridiculous may be defined as a mistake or deformity not productive of pain or harm to others." Thomas Hobbes explained that "the passion of laughter is nothing else but the sudden glory arising from a sudden conception of some eminency in ourselves by comparison with the infirmity of others, or with our own formerly." (Quoted in Arthur Koestler, *Insight and Outlook,* Macmillan, 1949, 56.)

The second "why" theory, and most widely held one, is *incongruity* theory which argues that laughter is created when there is a difference between what we expect and what we get. The punch line in jokes generates an incongruity that we find amusing. Schopenhauer describes what we call the incongruity theory as follows (Piddington: 1963:171-172) "The cause of laughter in every case is simply the sudden perception of the incongruity between a concept and the real object which have been thought through it in some relation, and laughter itself is just the expression of this incongruity."   In jokes, the sudden perception that Schopenhauer mentions is caused by the punch lines which generate this recognition of an incongruity. In a good joke, we don't know what to expect in the way of a punch line.

The third "why" theory is the *psychoanalytic* theory of humor which suggests that humor is primarily a form of masked aggression." As Freud wrote in his book, *Jokes and Their Relation to the Unconscious* (1963:101) "and here at last we can understand what it is that jokes achieve in the service of their purpose. They make possible the satisfaction of an instinct (whether lustful or hostile) in the face of an obstacle that stands in its way." (1963:101)." The wonderful thing about humor, from a psychoanalytic perspective, is that when we hear a joke we can participate in the aggression without any sense of guilt.

The fourth "why" theory ties humor to *communication paradoxes* and suggests that humor results from the use of paradox, play and the resolution of logical problems. As William Fry wrote in his book *Sweet Madness* (1963:158) "During the unfolding of humor, one is suddenly confronted by an explicit-implicit reversal when the punch line is delivered...Inescapably, the punch line combines communication with meta-communication." In the final analysis, these theorists argue that what goes on in jokes may be too complicated for us to understand at our present level of development. Now that I've discussed the four "why we laugh" theories of humor, let me offer a good Jewish joke.

A Priest, An Imam and a Rabbi Get a Haircut

This joke was told to me by a Jewish friend from Israel. I found it very funny and had a good laugh when I heard it but people who are not Jewish might not "get" it.

> A barber is sitting in his shop when a priest enters. "Can I have a haircut?" the priest asks. "Of course," says the barber. The barber than gives the priest a haircut. When the barber has finished, the priest asks "How much do I owe you?" "Nothing," replies the barber. "For you are a holy man." The priest leaves. The next morning, when the barber opens his shop, he finds a bag with one hundred gold coins in it." A short while later, an Imam enters the shop. "Can I have a haircut?" he asks. "Of course," says the barber, who gives the Imam a haircut. When the barber has finished, the Imam asks "How much do I owe you?" "Nothing," replies the barber. "For you are a holy man." The Imam leaves. The next morning, when the barber opens his shop, he finds a bag with a hundred gold coins in it." A bit later, a rabbi walks in the door. "Can I have a haircut?" the rabbi asks. "Of course," says the barber, who gives the rabbi a haircut. When the haircut is finished, the rabbi asks, "How much do I owe you?" "Nothing," replies the barber, for you are a holy man." The rabbi leaves. *The next morning, when the barber opens his show, he finds a hundred rabbis.* (Punch line in italics)

The problem with the "why" theories is they don't deal with the mechanisms in the joke I've just "told"--and we will be dealing with jokes here—short texts that generate the humor. I should point out that supporters of the various "why" theories spend a lot of time arguing with supporters of the other "why" theories about which theory is best.   But what is important, from my perspective, is that the "why" theories don't deal with the specifics of jokes to explain what it is, in a given joke, that evokes mirthful laughter. Superiority theorists would say we feel superior to the rabbi and the hundred rabbis who are crowded in the barbershop, hoping to get a free haircut. Incongruity theorists would say we are surprised by the punch line, though anyone familiar with Jewish humor might possibly have been able to anticipate the kind of resolution we find in the joke. Psychoanalytic critics would say the joke allows guilt-free aggression against Jews, who are the main protagonists in the joke and the subject of the punch line, and communication theorists would say the resolution is ultimately paradoxical and involves a communication, the punch line, and a meta-communication— laugh, but don't take this story seriously because it is a joke. But these "why" theories don't adequately explain what is going on in the joke.

Rather than arguing which "why" theory is best, I chose a different path. As the result of a large research project I conducted—a content analysis using all the books I had in my house with humorous content: joke books, books of folklore, comic strips, cartoons, humorous poems, theatrical comedies, humorous short stories, etc., etc. with a focus on what it was, in each text I examined, that was funny and that generated laughter. I came up with a list of 45 techniques which, I suggest, in various combinations, can be found in jokes and all other forms of humor. These techniques, we might say, are the DNA of humor. We often find two or three, or more, of these techniques in a joke. These techniques, I claim, inform humor from different time periods (for example, Plautus used them in his Roman comedies, Shakespeare used them in his comedies and Ionesco used them in his play *The Bald Soprano*) and in different cultures. I define and offer examples of humorous texts with each of the 45 techniques and then apply the techniques to humorous texts in my books *An Anatomy of Humor* and *The Art of Comedy Writing* and various articles that have been published in a number of journals.

.

What Makes Us Laugh: The 45 Techniques Found in Humor

After I came up with my list, I discovered that the techniques could be classified into four categories: jokes involving *language*, jokes involving *logic*, jokes involving *identity* and jokes involving gestures and similar *actions*. My list of techniques and their classifications follows:

Language	Logic	Identity	Action
Allusion	Absurdity	Before/After	Chase
Bombast	Accident	Burlesque	Slapstick
Definition	Analogy	Caricature	Speed

Exaggeration	Catalogue	Eccentricity
Facetiousness	Coincidence	Embarrassment
Insults	Comparison	Exposure
Infantilism	Disappointment	Grotesque
Irony	Ignorance	Imitation
Misunderstanding	Mistakes	Impersonation
Over literalness	Repetition	Mimicry
Puns/Wordplay	Reversal	Parody
Repartee	Rigidity	Scale
Ridicule	Theme/Variation	Stereotype
Sarcasm	Unmasking	
Satire		

45 Techniques of Humor by Category

In order to make these techniques easier to apply, I put them into alphabetical order and numbered them. This chart follows.

1. Absurdity	16. Embarrassment	31. Parody
2. Accident	17. Exaggeration	32. Puns
3. Allusion	18. Exposure	33. Repartee
4. Analogy	19. Facetiousness	34. Repetition
5. Before and After	20. Grotesque	35. Reversal
6. Bombast	21. Ignorance	36. Ridicule
7. Burlesque	22. Imitation	37. Rigidity
8. Caricature	23. Impersonation	38. Sarcasm
9. Catalogue	24. Infantilism	39. Satire
10. Chase Scene	25. Insults	40. Scale, Size

11. Coincidence	26. Irony	41. Slapstick
12. Comparison	27. Literalness	42. Speed
13. Definition	28. Mimicry	43. Stereotypes
14. Disappointmen t	29. Mistakes	44. Theme/Vari
15. Eccentricity	30. Misunderstanding	45. Unmasking

Techniques of Humor in Alphabetical Order

I will show how these techniques function in the joke about a priest, an imam and a rabbi who go to a barbershop to get a haircut. But first, we must decide what a joke is and then what makes a joke a Jewish joke.

Defining the Joke

I will define a joke as "a short narrative, with a punch line, meant to evoke mirthful laughter."

The narrative may have a number of events in it but if it is a joke, it will always have a punch line that is meant to generate mirthful laughter. The structure of the typical joke is shown below:

$$A \rightarrow \quad B \rightarrow \quad C \rightarrow D \rightarrow E \rightarrow F \quad \text{(punch line)}$$

$$\downarrow$$

$$G \quad \text{Mirthful laughter}$$

This diagram shows that jokes are short narratives and it offers an x-ray of the syntagmatic nature of this kind of text.   With this definition of the joke in mind, let me use my list of techniques to analyze the priest, imam and rabbi joke.

Techniques of Humor in the Priest, Imam and Rabbi Joke.

What follows are my suggestions about which techniques of humor are found in this joke. It is not unusual for a joke to make use of a number of different techniques.

Technique 44: Theme and Variation   (Logic Humor)

The first technique we find in the joke is 44, Theme and Variation. In *The Art of Comedy Writing* I define theme and variation as follows (1997:44):

> By theme and variation I refer to the technique comedy writers use to take some matter (a belief, an activity) and show how different nationalities, religions, occupations, members of social classes, etc. vary with regard to this belief or activity. Part of the humor here comes from seeing how the theme is varied by the different groups, and by the way this technique plays with stereotypes people have of the different groups.

There are three holy men and for most of the joke we find them doing the same thing—getting a haircut, asking to pay for the haircut but being told by the barber the haircut was free, and, for two of them, leaving the barber a hundred gold coins the next day. The three holy men are from different religions and the third holy man, the rabbi, doesn't leave a hundred gold coins but a hundred rabbis. That is the variation.

Technique 19: Facetiousness (Linguistic Humor)

In *An Anatomy of Humor*   I define facetiousness as follows (1993:34):

> Facetiousness is generally taken to mean a joking, nonseries us of language. There is an element of ambiguity, for the person does not really mean (or take seriously) what he or she says and this must be communicated one way or another...Facetiousness is similar to irony, but is weaker. In both techniques we must "read" or "decode" the message;   in irony there is a reversal, in facetiousness there is a discounting.

I understand facetious to mean a jesting, frivolous, nonserious use of language. The idea of having a hundred rabbis packed into a small barbershop is crazy and the joke's humor is based, in large measure, on the ridiculous nature of the idea.

Technique 1: Absurdity (Logic Humor)

I deal with absurdity in my *An Anatomy of Humor* and explain (1993:19):

> Absurdity and its related forms—confusion and nonsense—seems to be relatively simple, but it is not, and its effects may be quite complicated, as Freud pointed out in his discussion of nonsense humor. Absurdity works by making light of the "demands" of logic and rationality. This absurdity doesn't necessarily take the form of silliness (though in many children's jokes it does) but may be an example of a relatively sophisticated philosophical position....We all seem to need to impose our sense of logic and order on the world, and when we come across situations or instances where our logic doesn't work, we react by being puzzled and, in certain cases, amused.

I usually reserve the technique of absurdity to deal with the kind of plays one finds in the theater of the absurd, but it is reasonable to suggest that the idea of packing a hundred rabbis into a barbershop is absurd and that this absurdity helps generate the humor.

Technique 43: Stereotypes (Identity Humor)

My discussion of stereotypes, found in *An Anatomy of Humor,* relies on sociological theories about the subject. As I explain in my discussion of this technique (1993:52,53):

> Jokes involving stereotypes can be described as generalized insults—attacks on races, religions, ethnic groups, etc. but there is more to the humor of stereotypes than that. Stereotypes are useful to writers and comedians because they are instant (pseudo) "explanations" of behavior and they enable people to understand "motivation"....Stereotypes are, from a sociological point of view, group-held notions people have about other groups. Stereotypes can be negative, positive or mixed, but in all cases they are extreme over-simplifications and generalizations.

The joke also alludes to the stereotype that Jews are cheap—a stereotype that is widely held but also quite inaccurate. Instead of a hundred gold coins, the barber finds a hundred rabbis.

Technique 14: Disappointment (Logic Humor)

In my description of the humor of disappointment and defeated expectations in *An Anatomy of Humor* I write (1993:31):

> The technique of disappointment involves leading people on about something and then denying them the logical consequences they expect. It is very similar to teasing and is funny to the extent that we find minor disappointments amusing. A good deal depends upon the frame or situation in which the disappointment is staged.

The structure of the barbershop joke, with the first two holy men leaving a hundred gold coins, sets the listener of the joke up to expect that the rabbi will also leave a hundred gold coins. Instead, he "leaves" a hundred rabbis. This humor is based upon defeated expectations.

We can say the "formula" for this joke (that is, the techniques used in it) is: 44-19-43-14. Reducing a joke to a formula is, in itself, humorous. There are, in fact, jokes that use the idea of jokes having numbers to differentiate them from other jokes. For example, consider the following joke:

> At a conference of comedians, all the comedians know all the jokes so they now tell jokes by referring them to number. A comedian stands up and says "35-16-9-45" but nobody laughs. A comedian in the audience turns to a friend and says "he never could tell a joke well."

Now let us turn to a paradigmatic analysis of the priest, imam and rabbi joke.

The Paradigmatic Structure of the Priest, Imam and Rabbi Joke

In the "Introduction to the Second Edition" of Propp's *Morphology of the Folktale,* Alan Dundes writes (1968:xi):

There seems to be two distinct types of structural analyses in folklore. One is the type of which Propp's *Morphology of the Folktale* is the exemplar par excellence. In this type, the structure or formal organization of a folkloristic text is described following the chronological order of the linear sequences of elements in the text....Following Lévi-Strauss (1963:312) this linear sequential structural analysis we might term "syntagmatic" structural analysis....The other type of structural analysis in a folklore seeks to describe the pattern (usually based upon an a priori binary principle of opposition) which allegedly underlies the folkloristic text. This pattern is not the as the sequential structure at all. Rather, the elements are taken out of the "given" order and are regrouped in one or more analytic schema.

It was Claude Lévi-Strauss who suggested that the paradigmatic analysis of a text showed what it means in contrast to the syntagmatic analysis of a text, which shows what happens in it. We obtain the paradigmatic analysis of a text by finding the set of bipolar oppositions found (hidden) in the text.

I believe the basic opposition in this joke is between paying for a haircut and not paying for a haircut. We see this opposition in the chart below.

Pay for Haircut	Don't Pay for Haircut
The Priest, The Imam	The Rabbi
Ask How Much It Costs	Asks How Much It Costs
Each leaves 100 Gold Coins	Leaves 100 Rabbis

So this joke is about paying for haircuts and the punch line is about the way the Rabbi responded to the barber's statement that holy men don't have to pay for haircuts. It reflects an aspect of the Jewish psyche that offers an absurd resolution to the events in the joke. But what is a Jewish humor and what makes a joke a Jewish joke?

What is Jewish Humor

Freud said he knew of no people who made so much fun of themselves as the Jews and this joke reflects a common Jewish sensibility—to laugh at human foibles, whether they are in lay people or in religious figures like rabbis. This joke is an example of

Jewish humor, which we can define as humor in which Jewish people are the main characters and Jewish character traits and culture play an important role in generating the humor.

Avner Ziv, an Israeli humor scholar, defines Jewish humor and explains its origins in Eastern Europe. He writes, in his book *Jewish Humor* (1986:11):

> From my standpoint, a Jew is a man who considers himself Jewish and identifies with the Jewish people. Thus, Jewish humor can be defined as humor created by Jews intended mainly for Jews, and which reflects special aspects of Jewish life....Naturally, Jewish humor changes as a result of important changes in the life of the Jewish people. Thus, one can speak of Eastern European Jewish humor, Moroccan Jewish humor, American Jewish humor or Israeli Jewish humor. Nevertheless, what is identified in worldwide professional literature as Jewish humor originated in 19th Century Eastern Europe. There Jews lived under special and extremely harsh conditions confronted with a real danger to their lives. In these conditions, humor developed which had particular characteristics what helped the Jews cope with their terrible ordeals.

The fact that this Jewish joke has an Iman in it, instead of the characters we would find in earlier American jokes about holy men, namely a priest, a protestant minister and a rabbi, reflects important changes that have taken place in American culture and society. America is now a more multi-cultural, multi-ethnic and multi-religious society.

Conclusions

There are, in this joke, two other holy men: a priest and an imam. But the punch line involves a rabbi and thus I would suggest this is a Jewish joke. Many Jewish jokes involve people from other religions, ethnicities, races, countries, etc. But if the punch line involves Jews, it is generally safe to conclude that we have a Jewish joke. The rabbi in the joke wanted to pay for the haircut, but when the barber told him he didn't charge holy men for haircuts, the rabbi took advantage of his generosity and sent a hundred other rabbis to the barber. One could argue that the technique of literalness, technique 27, is also at play here since the barber told the rabbi he doesn't charge holy men for haircuts and that comment led to the punch line in the joke. The punch line, "he found a hundred rabbis," plays on our expectations that there will be a hundred something in the joke as well as the realization that if the rabbi left a hundred gold coins and nothing else happened there would be no joke. The fact that Jewish people are able to make fun of their rabbis, and often do in their jokes, suggests a different sensibility when it comes to relating to holy men and women (since there are now women rabbis) than you find in many other religions.

NOTE: This article was originally published in the European Journal of Psychology issue on humor.

References

Berger, Arthur Asa. 1993. *An Anatomy of Humor.* New Brunswick, NJ: Transaction

Berger, Arthur Asa. 1997. *The Art of Comedy Writing.* New Brunswick, NJ: Transaction

Berger, Arthur Asa. 1997. *The Genius of the Jewish Joke.* New York: Jason Aronson.

Fry, William. 1963. *Sweet Madness: A Study of Humor.* Palo Alto, CA: Pacific Books.

Piddington, Ralph. 1963. *The Psychology of Humor.* New York: Gamut Press

Propp, Vladimir. 1968. *Morphology of the Folktale.* 2nd Edition. Austin, TX: University of Texas Press.

Ziv, Avner. (Ed.) 1986. *Jewish Humor.* Tel Aviv: Papyrus at Tel Aviv University.

The present archival study examined the depiction of women's beauty in our society with respect to hair color, especially blondeness. Raters reliably categorized the hair color of cover models for two women's magazines (*Ladies Home Journal* and *Vogue*) and for *Playboy* magazine centerfolds from the 1950s through the 1980s. These media images from 750 observations were compared among magazines, among decades, and in relation to the proportion of blondes in a normative sample of adult White women. Results revealed that the percentage of blondes in each magazine exceeded the base rate of blondes in the norm group. Blondes were more prevalent in *Playboy* centerfolds than in the women's magazines. Although temporal patterns varied from magazine to magazine, the average proportion of blondes was lowest in the 1960s and highest in the 1970s. The study's findings have numerous implications for social issues and research regarding the psychology of physical appearance.

> Melissa K. Rich and Thomas F. Cash
> *The American image of beauty: Media representations of hair color for four decades*

Buy Scolds see, when they walk through the hair care aisle: a sea of items barely distinguishable from one another, with ungodly profit-margins built in, manufactured and marketed by male-dominated companies and their lackey ad agencies, whose mission is to spread insecurity and pit us against each other on the basis of whose hair is richer, softer, straighter, curlier, bouncier, or least likely to fly away.

> Lee Eisenberg
>
> *Shoptimism: Why the American Consumer Will Keep on Buying No Matter What*

Photo by Arthur Asa Berger

Was Medusa a Blonde?

The Semiotics of Hair Coloring for Women

The myth of the Gorgon Medusa is important in that it alerts us to the "magical" power of hair in Greek thought. Medusa was originally a beautiful maiden who was famous for her gorgeous hair. She said she was more beautiful than Athena (other versions say she violated Athena's temple) and was changed by Athena into a monster whose hair was made of snakes. Anyone who gazed upon Medusa was immediately turned to stone. She was killed by Perseus, who looked at her reflection in a shield and cut off her head. The message women take away from the Medusa myth is that hair is important and powerful and with the right hair style and the right hair color, it is possible to "kill" men's resistance and, so to speak, "knock 'em dead."

Mircea Eliade, the scholar of religion, pointed out in his book *The Sacred and the Profane,* that many of our contemporary everyday activities are camouflaged and degenerated myths and rituals that have been stripped of their sacred quality. So it is not too much of a stretch to tie the fact that countless numbers of women, all over the world, spend enormous sums of money, dying their hair or visiting beauty salons and having their hair styled and dyed…and they do this many times a year.

On Blondeness

"Many a blonde dyes by her own hand," it has been said, which refers to the millions of women who color their hair blonde at home. Relatively speaking, large numbers of these women dye their hair blonde because of the positive connotations of blondeness in western society, and now in societies everywhere. In his book *The New People,* sociologist Charles Winick has a discussion of hair color that sheds some light on our contemporary fascination with blondeness.

An Aside on Red Hair

He points out that in the United States, in the 1930's and 1940's, red hair was the most popular color for women. Many of the most popular actresses, such as Clara Bow, Maureen O'Hara, Greer Garson and Ann Sheridan, had red hair. The color red in women's hair was connected, in the popular imagination, with sin and sexuality. Red was, sexually speaking, a "hot" color. That changed and in recent decades, blonde has been the most popular color to dye one's hair.

I should mention that I am a redhead and that my red hair causes confusion with people. I was born in 1933 so I am a very senior citizen, yet my hair is red—not as bright a color as it was in my younger days, but still quite red. Actually, close to orange. My high school French teacher called me a "poil de carotte" or "carrot head." That was in 1948. My red hair leads to some speculation among people who don't know me personally as to how old I really am, though other signs of my age are quite apparent. I grew up in Boston and many people who saw me thought I was a little Irishman, though I happen to be Jewish. I've met people who didn't realize a person with red hair could be Jewish, though King David was, I believe, also a red head.

On a recent trip to Russia, I noticed that many older women in Moscow had dyed their hair red, except that the color was a ghastly red that looked like rusted steel wool. This is probably because they dyed their hair themselves and did a terrible job or went to hair salons that weren't very good. I couldn't help but wonder—do these women think their dyed red hair is attractive?

Perhaps they chose red because it is much easier to dye one's hair red than blonde, but I couldn't understand why they didn't choose brown or some other color that was easier to do.

Most of the women who dye their hair red end up with colors that are not pleasing, to my eye. It is a very difficult color to use, and one expert on hair color advises women to avoid the color. As Lois Joy Johnson writes in her article "The New Hair Color Rules," (*More,* July/August, 2007:68), quoting Brad Johns of the Elizabeth Arden Salon in New York City:

> If you're thinking red, go blonde. "Red hair, unless it's natural, is tough on mature skin tones," Johns notes. "It will expose and exaggerate blotchiness, brown spots or sallow undertones. But a honey blonde with golden tones works every time."

It only takes a single process to dye one's hair red but dying one's hair blonde requires two steps: first you must bleach your hair and then add the coloring.

The Semiotics of Blondeness

In Winick's book, *The New People,* he offers some suggestions about why blonde hair is so popular. He writes (1968:169):

> For some women, blonding is an opportunity to transcend their ethnic backgrounds. Others see it as a symbol of the child's light hair and towheadedness and for older women, blonding is a simple way of covering gray. There are some women who become blonde because changing hair is so profound an experience that they want a radically different hue. But for a substantial number of women, the attraction of blondeness is less an opportunity to have more fun than the communication of a lack of passion. One reason for Marilyn Monroe's enormous popularity was that she was less a tempestuous temptress than a non-threatening child. The innocence conveyed by blonde hair is also suggested by the 70 percent of baby dolls whose hair is blonde. D.H. Lawrence pointed out that the blonde women in American novels are often cool and unobtainable, while the dark women represent passion. Fiction blondes also tend to be vindictive and frigid.

In 1968, when Winick published his book, more than 20 percent of hair coloring preparations were for blonding while only 5 percent of American women were naturally blonde. Blonde hair color still is popular, and the number of women with dyed blonde hair greatly exceeds the number of women with natural blonde hair. Winick has many other interesting things to say about color, in many different areas—all to reinforce his basic thesis that sexual identity is becoming blurred in the United States, with males   becoming weaker and females stronger.   The subtitle of his book is "Desexualization in American Life" is really what the book is all about.

Grant McRacken, an anthropologist interested in hair color and related concerns has suggested that there is a typology of blondeness, with six categories of blondes. His work is described by Malcolm Gladwell as follows:

> In his brilliant 1995 book, "Big Hair: A Journey into the Transformation of Self," the Canadian anthropologist Grant McCracken argued for something he calls the "blondness periodic table," in which blondes are divided into six categories: the "bombshell blonde" (Mae West, Marilyn Monroe), the "sunny blonde" (Doris Day, Goldie Hawn), the "brassy blonde" (Candice Bergen), the "dangerous blonde" (Sharon Stone), the "society blonde" (C.Z. Guest), and the "cool blonde" (Marlene Dietrich, Grace Kelly). L'Oreal's innovation was to carve out a niche for itself in between the sunny blondes-the "simple, mild, and innocent" blondes-and the smart, bold, brassy blondes, who, in McCracken's words, "do not mediate their feelings or modulate their voices."
> http://www.gladwell.com/1999/1999_03_22_a_colors.html

What this typology suggests is that changing one's hair color is transformational and there are a number of different kinds of blondes and different colors for blonde hair; we cannot assume that all blondes are the same. These differences are often reflected in the women chosen to advertise the competing brands of hair coloring, with L'Oreal blondes being more upscale and sophisticated ("because I'm worth it") than Clairol's sunny housewives ("does she or doesn't she?"). Clairol's argument was that you couldn't tell that a woman had dyed her hair whereas L'Oreal, a more aspirational brand, was that the extra expense of using L'Oreal was okay because the woman dying her hair is "worth it." We have a battle here between disguise and narcissism.

A folklorist, Stanoy Stanoev, has interesting things to write about stereotypes of blondes in an article about blonde jokes titled "Dumb Blondes and Democracy." He writes:

> The choice of the Blonde is not a coincidence. Jokes manipulate an image already constructed in the masculine system of values and not just lately. As Marina Warner claims in her book "From the Beast to the Blonde: On Fairy Tales and Their Tellers," the fair color of hair and beauty have been conceptually connected in the visual and literature images even from antiquity, and it has lasting use since the 17th century up to the present day (see Thomas 1997: 285). The fair hair suggests purity and infantile innocence (Oring 2003: 63). This image still exists being broadly propagandized in public space during the 1920s, however, new connotations were brought to it – of sexual lust and temptation (Thomas 1997: 279), which in a far-fetched perspective suggests the idea of feminine fertility (Weigel 2006: 295). The combination between infantile innocence and sexual playfulness, attraction and even expertise began to characterize the Hollywood model embodied perhaps most completely by Marilyn Monroe (Thomas   1997:   279). http://www.folklore.ee/Folklore/vol46/stanoev.pdf

His article reprints a number of blonde jokes that have a sexual dimension to them. A large percentage of blonde jokes are not really jokes but take the form of questions and answers, with the answers functioning as punch lines and generating the humor:

> *Why is a dumb blonde carrying a mattress at the bus stop?*

> She has brought all necessary documents for a job interview.

> *Why don't dumb blondes go to church to pray?*

> Because kneeling down they automatically open their mouth.

> *Why do dumb blondes wear close fitting skirts?*

> So that their legs would not go apart.

These jokes can be seen as thinly disguised attacks on women and their role in modern societies. This question and answer format is common in insulting many jokes cycles about Poles, Elephants (stand-ins for blacks), JAPS (Jewish American Princesses) and other subcultures as well as racial and sexual minorities.

From a semiotic perspective, dying one's hair blonde means one is changing an important signifier and taking on a different persona or signified. A woman with dark hair who dyes her hair blonde reflects a semiotic puzzle. Her blonde hair, as a sign, suggests fun-loving innocence though also, at the same time, coldness and frigidity, yet she, as a dark haired woman (if D.H. Lawrence is correct) is passionate. Or, we might ask, does dying one's hair blonde suggest a change in temperament? This would mean that dark haired women who become blondes have undergone a change in temperament that they are unconsciously signaling to others by dying their hair blonde?

Here are some interesting statistics about hair coloring from www.marieclaire.com:

> **American Dye**: The U.S. is the home of the enhanced when it comes to hair color: Almost a quarter of women over 18 are blonde—by any means necessary.

> **TO DIY FOR:** $1.6 billion plus was spent in 2008 in the U.S. on at-home hair colorants.

We can see that the hair dying industry is quite large, for we also have to add the amount of money spent in the approximately 500,000 beauty salons in America. The salon business in the United States is a sixty billion dollar a year industry and spending on hair styling and coloring is now considered non-discretionary by many professional men and women, who feel (or have been taught by advertising agencies) that they must look good to get ahead.

Advertisements for home coloring products tend to focus on the "salon quality" of their dyes, on how long the coloring lasts, on their capacity to cover gray hair, and on avoiding flatness and dullness in hair that has been home-colored. Consider, for example, this copy from a Clairol "Nice n' Easy" advertisement:

> **Anti-Flat. Always dimensional home hair color.** Nice 'n Easy
> brings your look to life with depth and dimension. Our formula,
> with exclusive **Color Blend Technology**, gives every shade built-
> in tones & highlights so color will never be matte or flat.
> Permanent liquid hair color with Precision Applicator. Lasts up to
> 8 weeks. 100% gray coverage. Includes ColorSeal Conditioning
> Gloss to help seal in beautiful color and intense shine

The focus is on the lively and deep coloration, with tones and
highlights, that makes the hair beautiful and, for those using it to
color gray hair, its effectiveness in coloring gray hair. Hair color is
one of the few things that women (and men, as well) can easily
modify and lustrous, shiny hair color becomes connected, in the
collective unconscious, with youth (no gray hair anymore), beauty,
and femininity…and perhaps even fertility.

A British semiotician, Greg Rowland, suggests we find
"brand narcissism" at work in consumer cultures. As he explains in
his website:

> It's important for brands to be aware of the complexities and
> contradictions around the Consumer Narcissus. Consumer culture
> encourages consumers to think of themselves as special, unique
> and wonderful people. But this process, sometimes fueled by
> forms of over literal market research, can lead to a consumer
> tyranny wherein the hapless brand abandons core equities in knee-
> jerk responses to the whims of their consumer masters.
>
> We can never fully please the consumer. And this, ironically, is
> the key to the survival of the consumer economy. Consumer
> culture has constructed people that can never be fully satisfied by
> anything. But this infinite extension of desire is one of the pre-
> conditions for consumer culture to work effectively. We need to
> people to be relatively happy with their purchases, but not so
> happy that they don't continually explore new avenues of self-
> fulfillment through consumption. Consumer culture always leaves
> them wanting that little bit more, that indefinable something that
> will lead to genuine happiness.

Rowland argues that marketers have become dominated by research
that blinds them to the emotional needs people have and the way
they relate to products.

These marketers, he suggests, rely too much on consumer opinion and neglect the symbolic and semiotic significance of their products. He offers an example of a successful campaign, discussing the way L'Oreal sells its fragrances:

> The typical celebrity spokeswoman communication varies between a suggestion of friendly advice and implied threat. At stake is the very conception of yourself as Narcissus: "because you're worth it." L'Oreal builds up out idea of self-esteem, but threatens to take it away by non-participation in the brand. The consumer needs to echo the Narcissism of the brand in their own purchase of the product, otherwise they are left as an empty husk who, it is implied, "is not worth it." This continuing psychodrama between a Brand Narcissus simultaneously empowering and threatening the Consumer Narcissus has clearly worked very well for L'Oreal over many years.

This advertising uses consumer narcissism effectively and puts fragrance users in a psychological bind that works out very well for L'Oreal, for they must purchase the fragrance to demonstrate that they are "worth" it, otherwise they face a self-definition of not being "worth" it or very much else. The same argument applies to hair coloring.

Analyzing a Hair-Color Advertisement

This advertisement for hair color offers a number of interesting images. On the left side of the double-page advertisement, we see a the torso of a naked woman, with her elbows touching and her arms straight up holding what looks like a bunch of flower petals, with muted colors, in front of her face. She has long and lustrous red hair that cascades below her left shoulder. On the right hand page we read:

BEFORE, THERE WAS HAIR COLOR

NOW, THERE IS:

i n o a

EXCLUSIVELY AT YOUR L'OREAL SALON

PROFESSIONAL

Then we see a mixing implement and a brush and what seems to be a container in a soft light green spotlight and underneath that image we read:

NO AMONIA, NO ODOR

OPTIMIZED SCALP COMFORT

SUPREME RESPECT FOR THE HAIR*

INFINITE HAIRCOLOR POWER. SUBLIME SHINE

COVERS UP TO 100% WHITE.

> ODS Technology (oil delivery system): A breakthrough oil-based delivery system that maximizes the effectiveness of the permanent haircolor process, while providing 2X more lipid protection to hair, compared to our leading professional permanent haircolor brand in the world.*

There are then two footnotes in very small type at the bottom of the page about amino acids and hair's natural protective film--signifiers, I would suggest, of the alleged scientific nature of the product.

This advertisement offer sexuality and mystery on the left page. The woman is holding the flower petals in front of her face so we can't see her. Not having a face, it is possible that women can project themselves into the image. On the right hand side we find copy describing the hair color and an image that is difficult to see, with what seems to be a container all in shadows and a brush and mixing implement. The advertisement has a black background with the woman's hair and body highlighted and white or green type on the page with the copy. The woman's long red hair leads the eye to the copy about the product's features, which includes "sublime shine" and "covers up to 100% white."

Hair color advertisements attempt to do a number of things: inform women that the hair coloring product will not harm their hair or dry it out, that the color will last, and then assure them that their hair will be shining, radiant, soft, silky, lustrous and will remain that way for a long time.

On Brunettes and Blondes

According to Gossiprock.com (accessed 10/25/2011) brown is the most popular chair color now. As we read on the Gossiprock site:

> The latest hair-color trend is disproving the expression that blondes have more fun. You may have noticed a slew of hair-care products tailored toward brunettes, and that coincides with the strong popularity brown hair dyes are enjoying. Although brunette shades have always sold well, these days it is more chic to be brunette than to go golden, lighten to blonde, or tint your tresses auburn. Clairol and L'Oreal report increased sales for their entire lineups of brown hair dye, while salons across the country are reporting that brown is now the most popular color choice of clients, including natural blondes and redheads. Theories about what's behind this trend are numerous, ranging from simply following the trends of celebrities to society's perception that brunette women are more sophisticated and intelligent than blondes, and even to fashion's move toward blacks and earth tones, which are more flattering when worn by someone with brunette tones than by someone who is platinum blonde (Source: Wall Street Journal Online, June 3, 2005). I admit to being a part of this trend. Within the last year I have switched from light golden brown highlights to covering my gray with dark, chocolate brown hues. I find that it not only looks just as good but also involves less upkeep when roots start to show (and I am notoriously obsessive about my gray roots!).

> Gossiprock.com/forum

The popularity of brown coloring may be connected to the stereotype of the "dumb blonde" and all the dumb blonde jokes that were popular in the United States and many other countries in recent years. I have already offered some question-and-answer Blonde jokes.

We have to recognize that there are many stereotypes about hair color and that many women and men change their hair color due to colors worn by supermodels and celebrities and trends. Thus, the fashion of "blondes," which involves dark roots and blonde hair was made popular by the supermodel Gretchen Bundchen. Becoming a blonde provides either the best of both worlds—one is, semiotically speaking, both hot/passionate (dark hair showing at the roots) and cold/fun loving (blonde hair) at the same time. Blondness' can, by sending mixed messages, also signify confusion about one's sexuality.

Years ago, some young Japanese started dying their hair brown. This was taken as a sign of their alienation from Japanese culture and society. Now, there are large numbers of alienated young people in Japan, who dye their hair blonde, red and any other color they like. We also find blondes in other Asian countries and countries all over the world, where the color is a signifier of independence and, in many cases, alienation and anomie. Anomie is different from alienation in that anomie means, literally, normlessness while alienation refers to separation from the basic mores and values of a culture. It is possible to be alienated and anomic at the same time, of course. In the United States and many other countries, punk hair styles and hair colors—green, purple, blue--have become popular among many young people who are not necessarily alienated but are just enjoying the freedom societies now provides to express oneself. In this case, hair style and hair color become signifiers of "pinkness." We might wonder what the consequences of all this playing around with new hair styles and hair colors might be. Are we talking about relatively trivial temporary transformations of identity or something more long-lasting and profound? Let me offer a highly speculative hypothesis on this matter of dyed hair color with my discussion of impostors.

The Impostor: An Archetype

Whatever the motivations, dying one's hair is an example, semiotically speaking, of lying with signs—of being an impostor, and the impostor, I would suggest, is an important contemporary archetype.   Impostors   are   different   from   impersonators. Impersonators, as I understand the term, take on a given person's identity (for example, comedians imitating George Bush when he was the president of the United States) or different roles (truck drivers who pose as doctors) while impostors take on a different persona. Thus, brunettes who become blondes are impostors, as are all people who dye their hair different colors or cover gray hair with a color.

Many social scientists look at people in terms of aggregates--their memberships in groups, their gender or race or subculture or socio-economic class, or in terms of topics such as American national character or ideologies they adhere to, but our investigation of hair color suggests another topic—we must investigate how people arrive at themselves, at how they achieve their identities, or don't achieve them, since so many people are pretending to have an identity and are impostors. Dying one's hair blonde or red or whatever color is not a serious form of being an impostor, but people who dye their hair are impostors, nevertheless. In a society in which being an impostor is so prevalent, many people never grow up. They never cast off their immature notions and fantasies about what it is to be an adult, they never achieve continuity and coherence as a self.

These people cannot help themselves because they don't recognize that they are impostors. They've devoted all of their energy to fooling others and they end up, as we might imagine, fooling themselves, victims of their own duplicity. Many of these people suffer from a kind of amnesia about their childhoods, when many of the foundations for their identities were being formed, and their adolescent periods, when they were searching desperately for acceptable identities. Not knowing who they are, they are forced to continually   create   new   identities   for   themselves.   And postmodernism, with its attach on metanarratives, has only exacerbated the problem. Postmodernism provides a philosophical rationale for changing identities, and hair colors, on whims that people feel. Thus, we change the color of hair and our identities whenever we feel like doing so, leading to countless simulated blondes and red heads and brunettes—and contributing to what some theorists argue are decentered, fractured selves.

We don't know what color hair Medusa had. It didn't matter because anyone who looked at her was turned to stone. But this notion, that one's hair is powerful, lingers on in modern society in the psyches of all the women who focus their attention on their hair as an important signifier of their youthfulness (no gray hair showing) beauty and desirability. Beautiful hair—hair that is lustrous and shiny, with body, with rich coloration and luminescent highlights—does have a remarkable ability to enhance the way a woman looks and can have a considerable impact on others. There is an element of narcissism connected to this focus on beautiful hair and perhaps even a subliminal sense of panic in women who may have anxieties about being beautiful or not beautiful enough, a debased version of Protestant election that is exploited by companies manufacturing so-called "beauty" products.

If given the choice, I imagine that Medusa would have chosen to be a blonde. If being a blonde was good enough for Marilyn Monroe, it should have been, no doubt, good enough for Medusa.

References

Eliade, Mircea. *The Sacred and the Profane: The Nature of Religion.* 1961.

Transl. Willard Trask. New York: Harper & Row.

Winick, Charles. *The New People: Desexualization in American Life.* 1968.

New York: Pegasus.

Photo of Mosaic in Bardo Museum by Arthur Asa Berger

In the Labyrinth:

Interrogating the Advertising Image

In this chapter I will deal with two topics: first, visualizing dilemmas and second, some dilemmas of visualization, especially in the field of advertising. Since we are concerned with dilemmas of visuality, a question arises of some interest. How might we use visual images to illustrate a concept like the term "dilemma"?

Visualization of Dilemmas

I begin with a conceptual image from the great writer Jorge Luis Borges that can be found in his book *Labyrinths*. In that book he has a story, "The Garden of Forking Paths," and that title, I suggest, is a beautiful way to deal with the nature of dilemmas: a dilemma can be represented visually as a forking path. We confront various forking paths continually during the course of our lives.

Our lives can be represented visually as gigantic labyrinths, through which we wander—hoping, at each forking path, to avoid making serious mistakes and, above all, to avoid the Minotaur, a personification of disaster and death. Labyrinths are forking paths that lead to a center; mazes are forking paths without a center, through which one can wander endlessly..

Conventionally we understand the term "dilemma' to involve choices that are problematic. One of my dictionaries offers three definitions of the term:

1. Tragic one in which all choices are terrible.
2. Persistent problems
3. Two or more equally conclusive alternatives

In the labyrinth in Crete, the forking path always led to the Minotaur, who was imprisoned there by his father, the king of Minos. Every nine years the people of Athens were required to send seven young men and seven young women to Crete, who had to enter the labyrinth and who were devoured by the Minotaur. This situation ended when Theseus went as one of the seven young men, found the Minotaur sleeping, and strangled him with his bare hands. Other versions have Theseus killing the Minotaur other ways. And Theseus escaped from the labyrinth by following a thread that he had attached to the gate of the labyrinth and rolled out as he progressed through the labyrinth—a thread supplied by Ariadne, a goddess who fell in love with Theseus and who, according to some versions of the myth, he dumped a short while after finding his way out of the labyrinth.

Freud had an interesting psychoanalytic interpretation of the labyrinth. He writes, in his *New Introductory Lectures on Psychoanalysis* (1933/1965:25):

> I cannot resist pointing out how often light is thrown by the interpretation of dreams on mythological themes in particular. Thus, for instance the legend of the Labyrinth can be recognized as a representation of anal birth: the twisting paths are the bowels and Ariadne's thread is the umbilical cord.

Joseph L. Henderson, a Jungian theorist, had a different interpretation of the Labyrinth. He wrote in Carl G. Jung's *Man and His Symbols* that (1968:117):

> (In all cultures, the labyrinth has the meaning of an entangling and confusing representation of the world of matriarchical consciousness; it can be traversed only by those who are ready for a special initiation into the mysterious world of the collective unconscious.) Having overcome this danger, Theseus rescued Ariadne, a maiden in distress. This rescue symbolizes the liberation of the anima figure from the devouring aspect of the

mother figure. Not until this is accomplished can a man achieve his first true capacity for relatedness to women.

For Jungians, it would seem, we all must brave Labyrinths and deal with the problem of matriarchal consciousness just as for Freudians we must all deal with our Oedipal complexes.

There is another visual image we might consider that represents the concept of "dilemma" and that is from *The Odyssey,* in which Odysseus has a tragic dilemma to consider: if he sails too close to Scylla, she will seize six of his crewmen and devour them. But if he tries to avoid Scylla, Charybdis will suck his ship down into the sea and everyone will die. So Odysseus doesn't say anything to his crew members and sails close to Scylla, sacrificing the six to save the crew and himself.

Dilemmas of Visualization

Let me suggest that analyzing images is very much like traversing a Labyrinth and sailing between Scylla and Charybdis. Images are incredibly complex. What do we focus our attention on, as we scan them in a rapid series of saccades, and what do we neglect? How do we make sense of them? Every part of an image we examine, metaphorically sailing close to Scylla, means we have turned away from some other part of the image—avoiding Charybdis. We can cut this Gordian knot by examining all the more important parts of an image.

From the moment we wake up in the morning and open our eyes to the moment we fall asleep at night, we swim in a sea of visual images. And these images affect the way we see the world and act in it. Even at night, when we dream, we are intimately involved with images, for dreams are full of images that we later reconstruct, when we can remember our dreams, into a story. It is estimated that we get eighty percent of our information through our eyes. I am dealing here with visual images, not the kind of images found in articles such as "the image of the businessman in the twentieth century American novel" and that kind of thing. That is, I am concerned here with visual images, not mental constructs.

In considering the matter of dilemmas of visuality, it seems to be that there can be no better topic to deal with than advertising, a powerful form of visual persuasion of interest to us in print advertisements, television commercials and other forms of advertising found on the Internet and on mobile phones. There are a number of dilemmas to consider when we deal with the advertising image. One dilemma involves ethical choices made by companies and advertising agencies that attempt to manipulate people. Another dilemma involves the matter of how best to interrogate advertising images.

Since advertising is a means of persuasion, we must ask whether it is ethical for advertisers to use images to persuade people to purchase products or services that they don't need, they don't want, and, in some cases, are not good for them. This ethical dilemma involves using people as a means towards some end— greater sales for the companies making the advertisements—rather than treating people as ends in themselves. A related question involves whether it is ethical for advertisers to try to sell products or which are harmful to them, such as cigarettes and other tobacco products.

In the United States, some advertising agencies dealt with this dilemma by refusing to do cigarette advertising but most were happy to take on cigarette advertising. They argued "If we don't do it, someone else will, so it might as well be us." We have dealt with tobacco in the United States by outlawing advertising for cigarettes and most tobacco products.

There are related ethical problems: advertisers target adolescents for beer advertising that leads to drunkenness and in some cases alcoholism and many companies target children with sugary cereals and other foods that have contributed to the terrible obesity problem we face? The dilemma we face involves whether the government should allow this kind of advertising to continue or do something to curtail it. We can describe this dilemma as involving the right to "free speech" versus the need to protect children, adolescents and adults from communication that is unhealthy or destructive of their self-interest.

Interrogating Images

I used the image of a forking path as a means to show what a dilemma is. But what is an image? An image, as I define it, is anything that we see. More technically, from a semiotic perspective, an image is an assemblage of signs. And a sign is anything that can be used to stand for something else. As C.S. Peirce put it, a sign "is something which stands to somebody for something in some respect or capacity." Our task as interrogators of visual images is to find out what the image's story is. Sometimes the visual image tells us a great deal about the person who made the image and the society in which the image is found.

Images have the power to reveal our mental states. In my book *Seeing is Believing: An Introduction to Visual Communication,* I reproduce some drawings from a little girl, Betty, who was terribly disturbed. Her parents brought her to a therapist and also brought a number of her paintings, for she loved to paint. All of her drawings and paintings showed monsters and revealed a tortured psyche. As the therapy evolved, we can see how the paintings Betty painted changed, until at the end of her therapy, when she was cured, she made the kind of paintings a normal little girl would make.

If we are dealing with a photographic image with people in it, as is often the case with advertisements, we also have to learn to read the people as well as the other signs in the text. Images in advertisements and commercials have the power to create sexual desire, to convince people to purchase things, to make them want to visit tourist destinations, to vote for a politician, to remember national tragedies, to do all kinds of things. This means that people who create images have a certain responsibility for what they do. One dilemma that advertisers face involves their taking responsibility for their advertisements that have the power to shape behavior.

Advertisers want to help the companies that hire them grow but they do this by attempting to shape the behavior of target audiences, so they always find themselves caught between the Scylla of the demands of the companies that hire them and the Charybdis of the ethics of treating people as ends in themselves and not a means toward an end, namely greater sales.

There are some concepts from semiotics that are important to the analysis of visual images that I will be making. Let me offer four of them:

1.   Yuri Lotman on nothing being accidental in a work of art and texts having great richness and many meanings.

2.   Ferdinand de Saussure on how concepts are purely differential and take their meaning from oppositions.

3.   Charles. S. Peirce on the role of interpreters in finding meaning in signs.

4.   Umberto Eco on lying with signs.

Yuri Lotman wrote in his book, *The Structure of the Artistic Text* (1977:17) "the tendency to interpret everything in an artistic text as meaningful is so great that we rightfully consider nothing accidental in a work of art." This is an important point: everything in a visual image is important and conveys something of interest, but of course some things in an image are more important than others. He was writing about literary texts, but I think we can apply his notion to visual texts. Since an image can contain many things, I use the term "signemes" to deal with the signs we find in advertisements.

A second principle that we should consider comes from Saussure who explained, in his *Course in General Linguistics,* that concepts have no meaning in themselves but take their meaning from the system in which they are embedded. As he put it, "Concepts are purely differential and defined not by their positive characteristics but negatively by their relations with the other terms of the system." It is binary oppositions that generate meaning and we may say that the meaning of a visual sign comes from its not being its opposite.

Another important theory comes from C.S. Peirce and involves his well-known trichotomy of icon, index and symbol. Icons and indexes are relatively easy to understand but symbols are a much more complicated matter because their meaning is conventional. For Peirce, everything is a sign. As he wrote:

> It seems a strange thing, when one comes to consider it, that a sign should leave its interpreter to supply part of its meaning; but the explanation of the phenomenon lies in the fact that the entire universe…is perfused with signs, if it not composed exclusively of signs."

This means that semiotics becomes the master discipline, a notion that most semioticians would not dispute, and we all have an enormous amount of work to do to make sense of all these signs.

Finally, we must consider Umberto Eco's warning that signs can be used to lie. Signs substitute for other things but they also can lie. As he writes in his *A Theory of Semiotics* (1976:7) "If something cannot be used to lie, it cannot be used to tell the truth; it cannot be used "to tell" at all. This matter of using signs to lie is very common. That gorgeous woman you see in Thailand may very well be a transvestite; that blonde may really be a brunette; and that doctor you see may be an impostor who really is a truck driver.

I would also suggest that we must keep in mind the way scholars from different disciplines bring their perspectives to analyzing a visual image. In addition to semioticians, or perhaps allied with them, psychologists, sociologists, anthropologists and scholars from many other disciplines have insights we can use in analyzing a visual image. With these notions in mind, let's consider how to implement them and how to apply semiotics to interrogate a visual image.

When interrogating a print advertisement, there are any number of things to consider. Let me list some of them:

1. air style
2. Hair color
3. Eyeglasses and Sunglasses
4. Other props: earrings, nose rings, etc.
5. Teeth
6. Lips
7. Facial expression
8. Body language
9. Clothes worn
10. The design of the ad
11. Color used
12. Kind of shots

Let's consider the matter of facial expression.   One problem advertisers face is that they cannot be sure whether the people exposed to their advertisements are interpreting the facial expressions of the models in the advertisements correctly.   If you examine the examples of facial expression shown here by Paul Ekman, you probably would have trouble determining what each image represents.   In his research he found eight facial expressions that he claims are universal, but in many lectures I've given, people in the audience were unable to interpret the facial expressions correctly.

I will offer, now, a semiotic interpretation of two interesting texts: a Fidji print advertisement of a woman with a snake around her neck and the famous Macintosh "1984" television commercial.

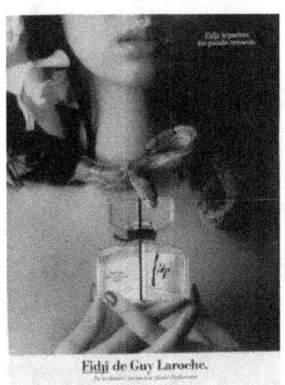

Fidji de Guy Laroche.

The design of this image is formal, based on axial balance. The image is relatively empty, with very little printed matter. The code for upscale products is simple and empty. The colors are warm, suggesting, perhaps, sexual passion.   We only see part of the woman's face, which enables women who view this image to project themselves into this scenario.   The woman seems to be Polynesian, evoking perhaps memories of Paul Gauguin escaping to paradisiacal Polynesia. Her dark hair suggests unrepressed sexual passion, in contrast to blonde hair which suggests innocence. She has an orchid in her hair, a flower being the sexual organ of a plant. There is a snake around her neck—a phallic symbol. It leads our eyes to the bottle of Fidji, which she is holding in a curious way, with her fingers interlaced with one another. The language is French, which in the American popular mind is equated with sexiness and sophistication.

The design of the advertisement is interesting. If you consider the snake to form something like an "S" and look at the three horizontal planes on the bottle as forming an E, and the fingers as forming an X, you get the word "SEX." And sex is what perfume is all about; its fragrance is "potent," functioning somewhat like venom in its impact on men.

This advertisement is meaningful to viewers because of the implicit oppositions it establishes in our minds. The interpreter, Peirce reminds us, supplies parts of the meaning of a text. Let me suggest, combining Saussure's insights about concepts being differential with Peirce's insights about the role of interpreters in making sense of a text, how viewers of this advertisement understand it, but suggesting the polar oppositions implied in the text.

Polynesian Woman	Caucasian Woman
Paradise	Boring ordinary life (Hell?)
Escape (Gauguin)	Imprisonment
Free Sexuality	Inhibited Sexuality
Magic	Rationality
Fidji perfume	Other perfumes

These oppositions are, we may say, built into the advertisement, for if concepts take their meaning through opposition, whatever we find in the Fidji advertisement takes its meaning from its opposite.

In the Western World, for people who are familiar with the Biblical story, a woman with a snake evokes the Myth of Adam and Eve. But there is a better myth involving snakes that is more pertinent. Let me suggest, then, that this advertisement is connected to a myth and this myth informs certain aspects of our cultural past. I offer, once again, what I describe as a "Myth Model" that traces a myth through the following areas:

a myth, generally from Greek, Roman or Biblical sourcest

psychoanalytical thought that employs the myth,

a **historical event** related to the myth,

a **text from elite culture** based on the myth,

a **text from popular culture** tied to the myth,

some aspect of everyday life based on the myth.

The myth I have chosen is Medusa, the Gorgon whose hair was made of snakes. Anyone who gazed upon Medusa was turned to stone. From a psychoanalytic point of view, with her hair of snakes, she was hyperphallic. For a historical act, we can take Cleopatra who killed herself with an asp. Her story was told in an elite culture text, Shakespeare's *Antony and Cleopatra* and various paintings of Cleopatra and books about her. In popular culture, we have the Fidji advertisement with the woman and a snake, and in everyday life, we have a woman who dabs on some Fidji perfume. The chart below shows the Myth Model and the Fidji Advertisement:

Myth	Medusa, the Gorgon with her hair of snakes
Psychoanalytic Theory	Hyperphallic nature of Medusa
Historical Aspects	Cleopatra kills herself with an asp
Elite Culture Text	Shakespeare's *Antony and Cleopatra*
Pop Culture Text	Perfume advertisement with snake
Everyday Life	Woman puts on Fidji Perfume

What this Myth Model analysis suggests is that a visual image's meaning is connected to the culture in which the image is found and, in some cases, to myths and fairytales. The culture and various other texts help supply some of the meaning of a visual image; its meaning is not exhausted in the signs found in the text. And, as we can see, many elite culture and popular culture texts and many aspects of everyday life also are connected to myths and various other texts that guide people. The dilemma that the "creatives" in advertising agencies face—the artists and copywriters—is trying to find a way to make sure their target audiences can decode their advertisements correctly.

I have shown how much there is in a print advertisement—a static image full of fascinating signemes: the orchid, the snake, the woman's lips, her fingers, the highlights on the bottle of Fidji, and so on. We can also use semiotics to interrogate images in television commercials, videos and films. Let me offer an example from one of the most interesting television commercials of recent decades—the famous "1984" Macintosh commercial directed by Ridley Scott.

This commercial was only shown once on national television, on the 1984 Superbowl, but it created so much interest that it was shown often on local television stations, which means it turned out to be relatively inexpensive in terms of the number of people who were exposed to it. The commercial cost $1.6 million dollars and won thirty-four national and international advertising awards and was described as "the commercial that outplayed the game."

In this commercial, a group of skinheads are shown marching in a column in a huge building, heading for a gigantic auditorium, where they are exposed to a doubletalk speech by a balding Big Brother figure, a bureaucrat on a gigantic television screen. We are obviously in a dystopian society where people are enslaved and brainwashed. Into this scene bursts a beautiful blonde woman running towards the auditorium, carrying a sledgehammer. She is pursued by guards. She races into the auditorium where the skinheads are seated, being brainwashed, and tosses her sledgehammer at the scream. It shatters and the skinheads gaze at it dazed and open-mouthed. Then we read:

On January 24th, Apple Computers will introduce the Macintosh

and you will see why 1984 won't be like "1984."

Scene for 1984 Macintosh Commercial

This shot shows the woman with the sledgehammer running into the huge auditorium where the skinheads are watching the lecture from one of the people who runs the place—in our mind, from a company the opposite of Apple, namely IBM. There are obvious mythic aspects to this commercial—calling to mind David defeating Goliath with a slingshot and a stone. The giant size of the person's face on the screen makes him a Goliath like figure. We must also consider that Apple's logo, an apple with a bite out of it, recalls the story of Adam and Eve and man's gaining knowledge.

We can analyze this image at a number of different levels:

The literal level.	A woman with a sledgehammer runs into a large auditorium.
The textual level.	This scene is part of a commercial and its meaning is connected to the events in the commercial.
The intertextual level.	The commercial calls to mind George Orwell's dystopian novel, *1984.*
The mythic level.	The story of David and Goliath in the Bible.

Here, again, we see that the meaning of an image is dependent upon both its place within the text and connections the image has to information the interpreter of the image brings to the image from a knowledge of literature and the Bible. So context, in a very general way, helps establish the meaning of this text just as the context of words helps establish their meaning. We can fit this commercial into my myth model as follows:

Myth	David kills Goliath with slingshot and stone.
Psychoanalytic theory:	Oedipus complex: little child, big parent.
History:	Sm all countries defeat bigger ones. USA Hockey teams defeats Russians in Olympics.
Elite Culture:	Statues, paintings of David.
Popular Culture:	1984 Macintosh commercial
Everyday Life:	Person buys a Macintosh computer instead of IBM

One of the ironies of history is that the Apple corporation, which positioned itself as supporting freedom and contrasted itself with IBM has changed and become very much like the Big Brother figure in the 1984 commercial, controlling every aspect of its customers use of media.

Conclusions

I have used semiotic theory to suggest how we can visualize the term "dilemma" and deal with the semiotic and cultural significance of Labyrinths, a fascinating print advertisement for Fidji perfume, and a prize-winning commercial for the Macintosh computer. I have shown how material outside of a text (in this case myths) often helps explain the significance of what is in the text and is needed to understand the importance of the various signs or signemes in the text. This poses a problem for those who create print advertisements and television commercials—what can they assume their target audiences know? I used to use the metaphor of myself as a "Secret Agent" looking for hidden meanings and that kind of thing in texts. Now I have found a new metaphor—we semioticians and cultural critics are all, I suggest, like Theseus, wandering around in a labyrinth, facing difficulties and dilemmas at every turn when it comes to analyzing a visual text, hoping we can get our work done before our confrontation with the dreaded Minotaur, the editor with the rejection slip or the nasty critic. Maybe it is the case that we interpret and analyze semiotically and live mythically.

Supergrow: Essays and Reports on Imagination in America: A Review

Supergrow is a collection of fifteen essays that appeared between 1966 and 1969 in publications such as *The American Scholar, The New York Times, Antioch Review, Esquire, Saturday Review* and *The Urban Review.* Some of the essays in the book originally appeared under different titles and some were revised for the book.

DeMott Sets the Tone for his Book

In the first paragraph of his Foreword, DeMott sets the tone for his book: (1970:11)

> The essays collected in this book are about everything under the sun—rock music, improving your sex, the Hollywood life, the uses of poetry, Marshall McLuhan, violence in Mississippi, group-grope theater, student revolts at home and abroad....And there isn't a unified tone or manner. Now the writer looks detached or even invisible; now he steps onstage and mugs a little; one minute he's in slippers in a study with fire and wine and cat (a relaxing ramble), and the next he's pressing an idea, selling something, obviously out to convince. Still, there is one kind of unity: most of the pieces keep turning a single simple idea, namely, that people ought to use their imaginations more.

That explains the subtitle of the book—Essays and Reports on Imagination in America. He concludes his Foreword with a passage that explains how his essays are to be judged and what his subject matter is: (1970:13)

> The case is that the arena in which to judge the worth of the sort
> of imagining most often spoken of in this book isn't literary (Jack
> is a better writer than Jim, etc.). The testing area is dailiness,
> ordinary human encounter, the supper table. And about the value
> of the imagination on that turf there really isn't any arguing: take
> the stuff away, and none of us, tads or dads, can live.

We learn from this passage that DeMott is not offering us a literary
work, evaluating the styles of various writers, but what might be
described as a sociological and political critique of various aspects
of everyday life in America—one informed by a powerful moral
sensibility and what might be described as an Emersonian sense of
self-reliance.

DeMott exhibits a refreshing unwillingness to "go with the
flow" and not get caught up in and go along with fashionable
intellectual fads like McLuhanism (or as some wit once put it,
McLunacy). I asked him whether he had changed his mind about
McLuhan in recent years and he wrote (Letter of August 15, 2002):

> About McLuhan: everybody owes vast amounts to him. I read
> BRIDE (*The Mechanical Bride*) shortly after it came out…the
> fundamental seriousness of the approach and the immensity of the
> subject discovered came through instantly. I hated the politics-is-
> over, end-of-history show boating that he fell into, and that
> became tragically influential, at least by my estimate.

Like McLuhan, DeMott took popular culture seriously—something
that was not in vogue in academic circles at the time, though things
have changed a great deal in recent years.

In his letter of August 15, 2002, he also described how he
became interested in pop culture.

> The answer to the question about when I started with pop is, of
> course, in high school…learning the music, listening to
> Leadbelly, Pinetop, playing in kid dance bands, etc. etc. Pop
> rhythms, whether words, pix, dance moves or what, owe
> everything to the music.

This passage helps explain DeMott's style. For a professor of
literature (he taught at Amherst college) he writes in a rather jazzy,
hip, literary- jargon-free manner. But his style does not deter from
the strength of his arguments, for in reading DeMott you find
yourself dealing with a thinker who is full of ideas and whose ideas

and arguments command respect.   He generally supports his contentions with strong evidence, and uses numerous quotations to buttress his arguments.

Reading DeMott is exhilarating, because he offers so many things to think about and because he offers some many insights into subjects of importance.   Whatever else you might want to say about DeMott, he isn't afraid to tackle some really tough subjects, about which many people are very touchy and in some cases passionate if not frenzied.   And so we find chapters on topics such as homosexuality   (the first chapter in the book), racism, rock, McLuhan, student rebels, and child-raising.

Other Books by DeMott

His most recent book, *Killer Woman Blues,* published in 2000, was described by Jonathan Kozol as "one of the most audaciously compelling works of social commentary I have read in a very long time."   And an earlier book, *The Trouble with Friendship* (1995) was lauded by Courtland Milloy in *The Quarterly Black Review of Books,* who wrote:

> DeMott's searing dissection of pop media culture lays out for his readers what is perhaps the most pervasive brainwashing scheme to be perpetrated on African Americans since slavery.   The disastrous consequences [include] deluding us into thinking that all whites have to do is be nice to blacks and all will be well.

You can see, from these quotations, that DeMott tackles very serious issues—but ones that are masked over, often, by a veneer of pop cultural mystification.

In 1966, four years before he published *Supergrow,* DeMott published *You Don't Say—Modern American Inhibitions,* another collection of essays from various publications (and now available from Transaction Publications, with a new introduction by the author).   In the introduction to the original edition DeMott offers his rationale for the book,   (2002:xxiii) "The pieces collected here harp on a simple truth: certain ways of feeling and talking that were once perfectly acceptable are now, in effect, forbidden."

The themes in *Supergrow* and *You Don't Say* suggest that in the 1960s DeMott was fascinated by two closely related deficiencies he found in American culture: our inhibitions that led to an inability to communicate and our lack of imagination—or, to be more precise, our unwillingness to use our imaginations more.

From the sixties to the present day, DeMott has continued to publish articles and books of social criticism—often tied to popular culture--along with novels and many book reviews. In his new introduction to *You Don't Say,* DeMott offers an important insight into his work. He writes (2002:ix)

> These essay were written in service—more or less—of a single theme, namely that nothing is as simple as it looks." His book is meant to be a corrective to lazy and sloppy thought, and to "dramatize that thinking and imagining usually stops to soon, misses one or another moral, social or historical relation, is under every slyer pressure to reduce, simplify, quit—and should, no matter what, resist the pressure.

This challenge, to think things through, to "think straight," and to reveal the conclusions to which this process leads—what has been described as "intellectual courage"--informs DeMott's writings.

At this point, I would like to say something about his background, so we can get a better idea of the man behind the voice crying in the western Massachusetts "wilderness" from the beautiful little town of Amherst, where he taught for forty years.

Benjamin DeMott's Background

Benjamin DeMott was born June 2, 1924 in Long Island, New York. He served in the infantry during the second World War, received a Ph.D. from Harvard in 1953, writing his thesis on philosophical languages in England in the 17th century. He taught at several black institutions, including Mary Holmes Junior College in West Point, Mississippi and Bethune Cookman college in Daytona Beach, Florida.

DeMott began teaching at Amherst College in 1951 and remained there, as Mellon Professor of Humanities, until 1991, when he retired. DeMott has also been a visiting professor of

American Studies at   institutions such as Yale, MIT, and the University of Birmingham in England.   He has also received two Guggenheim fellowships, various honorary degrees, and was a Fulbright professor.

He has published thirteen books and countless essays and reviews in publications such as *The New York Review of Books, Harper's, Esquire, Sociological Review,* and *the New York Times Book Review.* Among his recent books are *Created Equal* (1995) and *The Imperial Middle* (1990).

DeMott is married and has four children: Joey, Tom, Benjamin, and Megan.   He spends winters in Florida and summers in western Massachusetts.   He may be a "voice" crying in the wilderness—to the extent that western Massachusetts is a wilderness—but he has done a remarkable job of making that voice heard, and a good measure of his success is due to his style, that is, his literary voice, as well as the intellectual rigor of his arguments.

Why DeMott Taught in an English Department

There is a passage in *Supergrow* that explains why DeMott has chosen his base in an English department.   In his chapter "Reading, Writing, Reality, Unreality..." he writes: (1970:143)

> It is the place—there is no other in most schools—the place wherein the chief matters of concern are particulars of humanness—individual human feeling, human response, and human time, as these can be known through the written expression (at many literary levels) of men living and dead, and as they can be discovered by student writers seeking through words to name and compose their own experience.   English in sum is about my distinctness and the distinctness of other human beings. Its function, like that of some books called "great," is to provide an arena in which the separate man, the single ego, can strive at once to know the world through art, to know what if anything he uniquely is, and what some brothers uniquely are.   The instruments employed are the imagination, the intellect, and texts or events that rouse the former to life.   And, to repeat, the goal is not to know dates and authors and how to spell *recommend;* it is to expand the areas of the human world—areas that would not exist but for art—with which the individual man can feel solidarity and coextensiveness.

This statement can be looked upon as one of the charter statements behind the multi-disciplined approach in universities that has evolved in recent years that is called cultural studies. His definition of art is very latitudinarian—covering what we would call the popular arts as well as the so-called elite arts.

DeMott is interested in events and texts at many literary levels—from the elite to the popular—that rouse in him a need to explain their significance and that call for the exercise of imagination and intellect to do so. And his goal is a noble one...to help his readers gain a sense of solidarity and commonality with others. These goals, I would submit (and other reviewers of the book have made the same point) he achieves superbly.

It should be pointed out that in the early Fifties, what is known as "the New Criticism" championed by scholars such as Cleanth Brooks and Robert Penn Warren was in vogue. I was, from 1950 to 1954, an English major at the University in Massachusetts in Amherst and many of my professors were advocates of the "New Criticism," who had studied with Brooks at Yale. It argued, in essence, that a literary text should be seen as something divorced from social and political considerations and examined, essentially, in terms of its internal logic. Brooks and Warren had written a widely used textbook that explained their principles and used them to examine various works of literature.

Given this situation, DeMott has to be seen as a rebel He had the temerity to suggest that literature was intimately connected to social and political matters, a position that now is exemplified by cultural studies and by American Studies.

Postmodern thinkers, incidentally, have suggested that the old hierarchical distinction between "popular culture" and "elite culture" is spurious (as well as the boundary between art and everyday life) and that there is just art—some of which appeals primarily to one segment of a population and some of which appeals primarily to other segments of a population. And some of which just about everybody likes and some of which hardly anybody likes.

Supergrow

It is not my purpose, in this introduction, to discuss each of the fifteen essays in the book. That would require an introduction of awesome length and tedious complexity. Instead, I will discuss the chapter "Supergrow," which DeMott used as the title for his book. That would suggest the chapter has particular resonance for him.

Consider how he introduces the chapter. Let me quote the first paragraph of this essay: (1970:100)

> At first glance they look downright insignificant—the kid fixers, the Supergrow brainfood crowd. Their product says what is on the package, witness such hard-selling titles as these: *How to Double Your Child's Grades in School, How to Raise a Brighter Child, Give Your Child a Superior Mind, College Begins at Two, etc.* None of the authors is famous. (The big sellers are Eugene M. Schwartz, Isabelle P. Buckley, Siegfried and Therese Engelmann, and Joan Beck.) None holds a top establishment job. (Mrs. Beck's perch is the Chicago *Trib,* Schwartz is "in" Executive Training Techniques, Mrs. Buckley taught school in Hollywood and has some stars for fans, and Mr. And Mrs. Engelmann, the comers of the lot, fill a "research associates" slot in education at a making-it midwestern state U.) And as for the group's moral as opposed to pedagogical assumptions, they're as old as the Protestant Ethic—no ties with tricky New Thought—and rouse smiles as well as pain.

DeMott does a great deal in this paragraph. "At first glance they look downright insignificant" suggests that something has more importance that one might imagine. What he is dealing with, he tells us, is "the kid fixers, the Supergrow brainfood crowd."

His slangy language does not mask a sense that the subject of this essay—the "kid fixers" and the "crowd" that is capitalizing on the anxiety parents have about their children, are a bad lot. What they are peddling is a product with "hard-selling" titles such as *Give Your Child a Superior Mind* and *College Begins at Two.* The authors of these works are, in essence, a bunch of nobodies. "None holds a top establishment job," he asserts, and one couple, The Englemanns, are "research associates" as a "making-it" midwestern state U.—a place, no doubt, full of "making-it" professors and "research associates." DeMott's use of quote marks suggests that their affiliation with this university is not a strong one.

DeMott introduces the term "moral" next.   He ties the groups moral assumptions to the Protestant Ethic and their assumptions, he suggests, "rouse smiles as well as pain."   Anyone with a moral sensibility, DeMott suggests, cannot help but laugh that these people—who it is implied are, or are close to being, charlatans—are being taken seriously and feel pain at the damage their books are doing to children.   These books are also humorless, DeMott adds in the next paragraph, quoting from one of the authors who cites J. Edgar Hoover as her "spiritual authority."

Next, DeMott lists some of the methods his authors use in their books such as "Supergrow texts often favor sock-it-to-'em chapter heads," "pinpoint schedules of development suitable for nurseries in sci-fi flicks," "countless 'shut-up, he explained' situations, and "barkerese from which comic excesses regularly flow."   DeMott lets his experts self-destruct by quoting them, with telling effect.

Thus we read:

"Teach [your child] to read aggressively.   Actively. Tearing the ideas out of the pages with the techniques we are showing him in this book.

And:

By the time the child is 34 months old, he should know his capital letters perfectly....The child should learn to count to ten by the time he is 30 months...By the time the child is 3, he should know all the positions words...

and, miraculously:

In Florida, a fragile, dark-haired girl of forty-five months was reading a third grade book to her father, a surgeon.   Severely brain-damaged from birth and still unable to sit up or walk, Debbie had repeatedly been diagnosed as mentally retarded.   At two well-known medical centers her father had been advised to place her in an institution as a 'human vegetable.'   Yet now, although was not yet four, Debbie had a reading vocabulary that exceeded 1000 words.

These books are all part of the self-help phenomenon that is pervasive in America.

DeMott sees elements of Horatio Algerism in these books (what he calls "the bootstrap myth") and a kind of over-ambitiousness that is projected by people on their young children. But there's more to them than that. As he explains, Supergrow also has bearings "on themes as large as that of Individualism and the Family," (1970:106) which is profoundly affected by the standardization that is influencing every aspect of contemporary American life and the flight from it by many people.

As he writes: (1970:108)

> When parents take upon themselves responsibility for school learning, when they announce that their account of their child's strengths, weaknesses, feelings, correct temper, and occupation precisely jibes with that of the school, when in short they behave in a manner implying that the home is but an adjunct of the school, yet another subtle erosion of the imagination of difference occurs. The child takes the cultural winds straight on his bow and hangs defenseless, unable to set courses of his of his own. He perceives that his father, when most intentionally concerned with him, is in fact a mere extension of school people who have no private involvement of feeling with him...

And now we see that DeMott's inquiry, which seemed at first to be dealing with trivial matters, is actually dealing with concerns of the utmost importance. He then writes "*á bas* Supergrow," pointing out that he has taken this line (and the title of his essay) from a book by Eda Le Shan, *The Conspiracy Against Childhood,* which he describes as "a ferocious assault on early learning."

He discusses his experiences teaching disadvantaged black kids in Washington DC and then, teaching white suburban children of the same age. This leads him to meditate on the utility of teaching disadvantaged black children the same things that white middle-class children learn. The black children, he says, breathe more easily and have "more participatory energies" and "more appetite" than the white children, who he describes with terms such as "more wariness, less response, sadness in their lucky middle-class eyes." He wonders whether the "disadvantaged" should be required to recapitulate the experience of middle-class white kids, and what will happen if black kids don't do this.

This leads him to a wonderful quotation from Dr. Johnson. "You teach your daughters the diameters of the planets and wonder when you have done that they do not delight in your company." DeMott concludes with a statement of what he thinks the aims of education should be:

> We need to remember, that is to say, that we seek something more than proficiency *or* privacy *or* preparation for next year's objective tests. We want appetites and responsiveness, a feeling of personal unity and togetherness, belief in the possibility of meeting a problem by using the mind, openness to pleasures that can spring as easily from a "shocking" dirty word shared at age forty around the supper table, as from a thousand-word vocabulary picked up at three. We want competency and self-reliance which, while not unrelated to manipulative skills, derive less directly from them than from the habit of inquiry into connections among visible bits of experience, keen practice at exploring "the working of each part on every part of the common life of men."

This, and not the nonsense perpetrators by the writers of Supergrow books, is what is necessary—children who are exhilarated by learning rather than robots who have been force-fed vocabularies and whose imaginations and sense of vitality have been deadened.

Conclusions

What we find in this essay is typical of what we find in the other essays in *Supergrow*. DeMott takes subjects which may seem, at first glance, trivial and of minor significance, but finds in them issues of major importance. He is able to read, at Blake put it, "the universe in a grain of sand." One of the things that informs DeMott's writing is his moral sensibility, his sense of outrage at some of the things that are done to children, to blacks, to women, and others who have been victimized, one way or another, in American society.

DeMott is what I would call, taking the term from Musil, a "possibilitiarian." Musil discusses people who have a sense of possibility in his monumental novel *The Man Without Qualities*. He writes: (1965:12)

> Anyone possessing it does not say, for instance: Here this or that has happened, will happen, must happen. He uses his imagination and says: Here such and such might, should, or ought to happen.

> And if he is told that something *is* the way it is, then he thinks:
> Well, it could probably just as easily be some other way. So the
> sense of possibility might be defined outright as the capacity to
> think how everything could "just as easily" be, and to attach no
> more importance to what is than to what is not....Such
> possibilitarians live, it is said, within a finer web, a web of haze,
> imaginings, fantasy and the subjunctive mood. If children show
> this tendency it is vigorously driven out of them, and in their
> presence such people are referred to as crackbrains, dreamers,
> weaklings, know-alls, and carpers and cavillers.

Somehow or other, Benjamin DeMott maintained his sense of
possibility that, if Musil is correct, probably began when he was
very young. DeMott continued to believe that things could be
otherwise and better, and he has worked for some forty years to
make a difference.

There is one other literary figure whose ideas are relevant
here—and I have taken the liberty of using literature in this
Introduction because we are dealing with an English professor and a
writer.

In his "Essay on Man," Alexander Pope, one of the great
literary masters of the English language, wrote:

> All Nature is but art, unknown to thee;
>
> All chance, direction, which thou canst not see;
>
> All discord, harmony not understood;
>
> All partial evil, universal good:
>
> And, spite of pride, in erring reason's spite,
>
> One truth is clear: Whatever IS, IS RIGHT.

DeMott, quite obviously, didn't agree with this perspective on
things, and explained why in his many articles and books. And we
are all much the better for it.

Books by Benjamin DeMott

You Don't Say: Modern American Inhibitions. Transaction. 2002

Killer Blues: Why Americans Can't Think Straight about Gender and Power.

2000. Houghton Mifflin.

The Trouble with Friendship: Why Americans Can't Think Straight about

Race. 1998. Yale University Press.

Created Equal: Reading and Writing About Class in America. 1996.

Addison-Wesley.

Business Self: The Recovery of Public Esteem.   1993.   Baruch College

of the City University of New York.

The Imperial Middle: Why Americans Can't Think Straight About Class.

1990. William Morrow.

Close Imagining: An Introduction to Literature. 1987. Bedford/St. Martin's.

Surviving the 70's. 1971. E.P.Dutton.

Supergrow: Essays and Reports on Imagination in America. 1970.

Delta.

Tourists as Consumers, Consumers as Tourists

Perspectives on Tourist Motivations and Preferences

More and more people are becoming international tourists. International tourism continues to grow unabated. Cruise companies are building gigantic cruise ships now—some that hold more than 4000 people and the airlines have increased their international flights over the years. While it is relatively easy to count the number of tourists, it is far more difficult to ascertain why people become tourists and why they select particular destinations and tourism products.

Tourism is a form of consumption that involves expenses of varying kinds. Tourists, especially international tourists, find themselves with needing to purchase transportation to wherever they are going and once they have arrived at their destination they must spend money for accommodation, food, drinks, entry tickets to attractions and all kinds of other things. To visit some countries they must also purchase an entry visa, which is an additional expense. A useful image describing the consumption aspects of tourism would be of a group of tourists being circled by a retinue of people that they she must employ—travel agents, merchants who sell suitcases and other kinds of travel gear, airline company clerks and reservation agents, porters, cab drivers, waiters in restaurants, guides at destinations, and hotel clerks, to name just a few.

Leisure tourism, then, is an important part of modern consumer culture that involves many related secondary kinds of consumption. Research evidence shows that one of the main activities tourists engage in is shopping (U.S. Travelers to Overseas, January-December, 2005. "In Flight Survey," International Trade Administration, Office of Travel and Tourism Industries. United States Department of Commerce.) , so consumption also plays a major role not only in tourist's choices of places to visit but also in their activities when traveling.

I address here several different concepts and theories that can explain consumer behavior and which can be applied to one particular kind of consumption—that of tourists. The focus is upon American consumer culture and tourism but the concepts and theories discussed can be used to analyze tourists as consumers in other countries as well. Tourist motivation for travel has been investigated by many scholars over the years but the argument of this paper, based on grid-group theory, is that there is not one consumer culture or one touristic consumer culture but four different consumer cultures that can be found in all modern societies. This means there are four different kinds of tourists based on their association with one of four cultural groups, or what the social anthropologist Mary Douglas calls "lifestyles (Douglas and Isherwood 1979).

Before discussing grid-group theory, this paper deals with a number of other approaches to consumer culture, all of which have implications for tourism and most of which will be related to tourist preferences. We begin with a psychological profile of consumption by psychologist Barry Schwartz (2004) as elaborated in his book *The Paradox of Choice,* and in a number of his articles.

Maximizers and Satisfizers

According to Schwartz (2004:4), consumers have become overwhelmed with choices in many areas. Schwartz notes:

> One day I went to the GAP to buy a pair of jeans. A salesperson asked if she could help. "I want a pair of jeans—32-28," I said. "Do you want them slim fit, easy fit, relaxed fit, baggy or extra baggy?" she replied. "Do you want them stone-washed, acid-washed, or distressed? "Do you want them button-fly or zipper-fly? Do you want them faded or regular?

He points out that in addition to the numerous kinds and styles of jeans, there are now eighty types of painkillers and forty kinds of toothpaste. One could add Starbucks to this list where the request for a cup of coffee gets the reply: what kind? This is followed by a list of choices including espresso, cappuccino, latte or even pumpkin spiced latte leaving the average coffee drinker highly confused. This paradox of choice, Schwartz suggests, has led, ironically, to a decreased sense of wellbeing. Thus "increased choice and increased affluence have, in fact, been accompanied by decreased well-being…As we become freer to pursue and do whatever we want, we get less and less happy." These feelings are due, in part, to unrealistic expectations we have about every aspect of our lives (Schwartz 2004).

We can see how Schwartz's work can be applied to the dilemma potential holiday makers face in selecting destinations to visit and to the problems and disappointments tourists may experience due to their inflated and unrealistic expectations of the experiences they hope to gain at the destination. A visit to ITB in Berlin, the world's largest tourism exchange, will find the consumer overwhelmed by the representatives of almost all countries and regions of the world. From Afghanistan to Zambia and from abseiling to Zodiac cruising the choice of holiday destinations and activities is endless and highly confusing. Schwartz (2004) explains that there are two kinds of shoppers -- what he calls "maximizers" and "satisfizers". The main components of Schwartz's theory are outlined below and then the authors suggest how the two kinds of consumers are likely to function as potential tourists. Schwartz characterizes his two kinds of consumers as follows: *Maximizers* must have the very best, have high expectations and face great stress and anxiety. In contrast *Satisfizers* think that good enough is acceptable, have low expectations and are at ease and relaxed.

When Schwartz's theory is applied to types of tourists we can suggest that the *Maximizers* focus on exclusive destinations and visitor attractions; they are annoyed when things go wrong but money is not an issue. They do, however, get upset when they feel that they have paid too much for a good or service. In contrast the *Satisfizers* are more attracted to mass tourism products, in particular relatively low cost all-inclusive packages. They have a flexible attitude towards their holiday experiences and are in general relaxed about travel expenses. Schwartz's two kinds of consumers are, of course, extremes and polar opposites; many consumers and tourists probably fall in various spots between the two polarities.

Culture Codes and Tourism

In his book *The Culture Code: An Ingenious Way to Understand Why People Around The World Live and Buy as They Do* (Rapaille, 2006) offers another perspective on tourist preferences, based upon the notion that when children grow up in a particular culture they learn certain codes that shape their thinking and behavior. Rapaille, a psychoanalyst and marketing expert, defines a culture code as "the unconscious meaning we apply to any given thing—a car, a type of food, a relationship, even a country— via the culture in which we are raised." (2006:5). He argues that there are three variations of the unconscious: the Freudian individual unconscious, which guides individuals; the Jungian collective unconscious, which guides all human beings; and the cultural unconscious that is based on specific cultures, and more importantly, on nationalities, which, his theory asserts, have their own mind-sets. These mind-sets, in profound ways, teach people who they are and generate the codes, the action principles, which are based on each distinctive national cultural unconscious.

Rapaille suggests that traditional surveys and other similar means of gauging public opinion are not helpful, for a number of reasons. His research is guided by five principles. First, he explains, "You can't believe what people say." This is because people often give you the answers to questions that they think you want and, in addition, because "most people don't know why they do the things they do." (2006:14).

His second principle states that "Emotion is the energy required to learn anything." Emotions, he suggests, are the keys to learning and to being imprinted with cultural codes, and, he adds, most of this imprinting is done while we are children, up to the age of seven. His third principle is "the structure, not the content, is the message," and in this respect he refers to the work of the anthropologist Claude Lévi-Strauss. When Rapaille examines statements written by participants in "discovery sessions" (to be explained below) he looks for what he calls structural phenomena, or themes.

This leads to his fourth principle which states "There is a window in time for imprinting [generally during the first seven years of a child's life] and the meaning of the imprint varies from one culture to another."(2006:21) Rapaille's fifth principle is that "to access the meaning of an imprint with a particular culture, you must learn the code for that imprint." (2006:24) That turns out to be the key to his approach—examining cultures for their unconsciously generated and imprinted codes which help explain why members of particular national cultures live and consume the way they do. Rapaille offers an interesting example of the way these codings work. The French code cheese as "alive," and to keep it alive, they store it at room temperature in a cloche. Americans, on the other hand, code cheese as "dead," and, since it is dead, they place it in plastic and in "a morgue also known as a refrigerator." (2006:25.)

Rapaille brings "discovery groups" of people together for three hours. In the first hour, he assumes the role of the "stranger." He pretends he knows nothing about whatever product he is investigating and asks members of the discovery group he has assembled to help him understand the product. The assumption he makes is that the contributions of the members of his discovery group will provide him with valuable insights into the codes that shape their behavior. In the second hour, members of his discovery group sit on the floor and cut out words from magazines that they use them to make a collage of words about the product. In the third hour, he has the members of the group lie on the floor, with their heads on pillows, while he plays soothing music. This is to induce them to reach a tranquil stage just before sleep, when they can, he asserts, return to the first imprints that were made on them about the product being considered. He asks them to recall their first memory of the product and the emotions they felt about it. They write comments about these emotions that he uses to discern the codes that are relevant to the product. He explains his theory as follows:

> If I could get to the source of these imprints—if I could somehow
> 'decode' elements of culture to discover the emotions and
> meanings attached to them—I would learn a great deal about
> human behavior and how it varies across the planet. This set me
> on the course of my life's work. I went off in search of the Codes
> hidden with the unconscious of every culture. "(2006:10).

Though we have a common humanity people really are different in
terms of their national cultures, Rapaille argues, and the culture code
is the means by which he can understand these differences.

Rapaille discusses a subject of importance to the hospitality
side of the tourism industry: the way people relate to food, and he
does so using a comparative perspective to focus on different
national cultural codings. Thus, in dealing with a subject, such as
what dinner "means" to Americans, he also discusses dining in other
countries, such as England, France, and Japan. In his search for
culture codes, he relies exclusively, it would seem, on written
statements from the people who participate in his "discovery"
sessions. He typically quotes from a number of representative
statements and then derives his codes from these statements.

In the section on "More is More: The Codes for Food and
Alcohol," he describes codings for food in America, but he also
deals with codings for food in France, and Italy. Rapaille offers six
quotations from his discovery sessions about food which provide
him with information about the way Americans are "coded" for
food. He says he recognizes that there are many people interested in
fine dining and good food in America, commonly known as
"foodies," but the message he got from the stories his respondents
during a discovery session on food wrote about was that our bodies
are machines and food is what we need to keep the machine
running. Thus, he asserts: "The American Culture-Code for food is
FUEL." Since Americans see food as fuel, they tend to end a meal,
Rapaille suggests, saying "I'm full" while French people, he
asserts—based on having grown up in France where the imprinting
and coding are different--typically end a meal by saying: "That was
delicious." Rapaille recognizes that every culture is full of tensions,
caused by conflicting archetypes.

Anthropologist Ruth Benedict asked what it is that makes
Japan a nation of Japanese, the United States a nation of Americans,
France a nation of Frenchmen, Russia a nation of Russians.

Rapaille's answer is that it is the codes that shape each of the cultures and the individuals who grow up in each culture and he offers some intriguing and suggestive insights into how people arrive at their national-cultural identities. Tourism professionals can take the concept of national codings for food, travel, recreation, sex and other matters and use these codings in designing hotels, planning tours and creating attractions.

The Disney Corporation made serious errors in planning its Disneyland in Paris by not allowing sufficient space or time for French people to dine the way they are accustomed to dining which includes the consumption of wine with their meals. On the other hand, since Americans, as a rule, regard food as fuel, fast food and similar operations are perfectly acceptable to most Americans at most sites of touristic interest in the United States and the fact that no alcohol is served in fast food outlets does not cause concerns for the American consumer.

Four and Only Four Kinds of Tourists: Grid-group Theory

Grid-group theory was elaborated by social anthropologist Mary Douglas in a number of articles and books and a work in which she collaborated with political scientist Aaron Wildavsky, *Risk and Culture.* (Douglas and Isherwood 1979); (Douglas and Wildavsky 1982). One of her more recent works, a seminal essay on grid-group theory and consumer behavior, "In Defence [sic] of Shopping" (1997) is of particular interest because of its implications for tourism studies. Another important explanation of grid-group theory is found in Thompson, Ellis and Wildavsky (1990), *Cultural Theory* and Wildavsky's article, "Choosing Preferences by Constructing Institutions: A Cultural Theory of Preference Formation" (1987). In this article, based on his presidential address to the American Political Science Association, Wildavsky offers an explanation of the basis for grid-group theory. He writes:

> The dimensions of cultural theory are based on answers to two questions: Who am I? and What shall I do? The question of identity may be answered that individuals belong to a strong group, a collective, that makes decisions binding on all members or that their ties to others are weak in that their choices only bind themselves. The question of action is answered by responding

that the individual is subject to many or few prescriptions, a free spirit or a spirit tightly constrained. The strength or weakness of group boundaries and the numerous or few, varied or similar, prescriptions binding or freeing individuals are the components of their culture. (Quoted in Arthur Asa Berger, Ed. *Political Culture and Public Opinion,* 1989:25. Transaction Publishers.)

The chart below shows how the strength or weakness of group boundaries and the number and variety of rules and prescriptions yields four groups, whose names have changed over the years. Wildavsky has used designations such as "Hierarchical Elitists," "Competitive Individualists," "Fatalists," and "Egalitarians" as well as other terms in his work involving grid-group theory.

Group Boundaries: Strong or Weak	Grid Aspects: Kinds and Number of Prescriptions	Way of Life Consumer Cultures
Strong	Numerous and Varied	Elitist
Weak	Numerous and Varied	Fatalist (Isolates)
Strong	Few or Minimal	Egalitarian (Enclavists)
Weak	Few or Minimal	Individualist

Individualists, Wildavsky adds, favor self-regulation, bidding and bargaining to minimize the need for authority, and want a minimum of interference from external sources. Hierarchists believe in stratification because they see it as functional, enabling people to live with one another in greater harmony. Egalitarians focus their attention on the needs that all people have and on minimizing the differences between people. They tend to function as critics of the social order arguing that inequality is mainly the product of corruption and duplicity. Fatalists are apathetic because they cannot control what happens to them, in part due to the fact that rather strong restrictions are imposed on them by external forces.

In their book *Cultural Theory* (Thompson et al 1990) explain that the elitists and individualists are the basic or dominant groups in societies, with the egalitarians functioning as critics of the status quo and the fatalists generally lingering at the bottom of the ladder. The book deals with an interesting question related to this matter of consumer preferences—are people free? Thompson, Ellis and Wildavsky (1990:13) explain that categorizing people seems to do violence to their individuality, since it suggests that their ways of life program them and they become little more than robots, ciphers or windup toys. Thus preference choice based on lifestyles and groups seems to preclude individual choice.   They argue that the different ways of life offer individuals a good deal of choice, since people can move from one lifestyle to another.

If the lifestyles aren't providing satisfaction or "payoff" people adopt different lifestyles and change political cultures. Thompson et al (1990) also point out something important for our purposes. They write, "a further virtue of the grid-group framework is that the categories are formed from dimensions rather than being derived ad hoc from observation" (1990:14). The problem with ad hoc categories, they argue, is that they are formed to fit observations and thus they generate uneven typologies.

As a political scientist, Wildavsky (1989) was interested in the four groups as political cultures and argued that it was membership in one of the four political cultures that explained political behavior and voting more adequately than concepts such as self-interest, which has been the dominant approach of political scientists. Even though members of a particular culture or people leading one of the four lifestyles may not be able to articulate their beliefs and values in great detail and are not aware of the fact that they belong to one of the four political cultures or grid-group lifestyles, they can recognize that their values and beliefs aren't those of members of the other consumer cultures.

This has important implications, for it means that consumption is primarily based on cultural alignments and hostilities and not on individual wants or desires. Consumer preferences are not based on personality but on membership in one of the four consumer cultures or "lifestyles" and antagonism toward the other consumer cultures. Grid-group theory postulates a fifth way of life, autonomy, but this group is very small, made up of "hermits," who are unlikely to travel and, as such, is not of concern to us and to tourism.

To see how the four cultures or grid-group lifestyles lead to consumer choices, we can examine how they shape preferences in the mass media. Members of each grid-group lifestyle would logically be attracted to certain mass mediated texts and repelled by others. We can assume two things: first, *reinforcement theory* tells us that people wish to reinforce their beliefs and thus search for material that is congruent with their values; second, *cognitive dissonance theory* tells us that people wish to avoid dissonance and thus avoid films, television programs and other texts and experiences that conflict with and challenge their beliefs and other matters connected with their identification with one particular grid-group lifestyle or political culture.

We can take songs to show how the lifestyle preferences work. Elitists would like "God Save the Queen," individualists would like "I Did It My Way," Egalitarians would like "We are the World," and Fatalits would like songs like "Anarchy in the UK."

Douglas makes an important point in her analysis of shopping that has profound implications for the study of tourist preferences. She writes, in here essay "In Defence of Shopping": that

> We have to make a radical shift away from thinking about consumption as a manifestation of individual choices. Culture itself is the result of myriads of individual choices, not primarily between commodities but between kinds of relationships." (1997:17)

The most important choice an individual has to make involves deciding what kind of a society, group, or in her terms "lifestyle" to associate with. Once that choice is made, everything else follows from it. As she explains,   Artefacts are selected to demonstrate the choice.

> Food is eaten, clothes are worn, cinema, books, music, holidays, all the rest are choices that conform with the initial choice for a form of society. Commodities are chosen because they are not neutral; they are chosen because they would not be tolerated in the rejected forms of society and are therefore permissible in the preferred form. Hostility is implicit in their selection."(1997: 18)

It is, then, the grid-group lifestyles that shape our consumption choices, and not personal taste, personality or other matters that are generally considered to be determinative when considering consumer preferences.

And it is their mutual hostility, Douglas adds, that accounts for the stability of the four competing lifestyles; they are all based on organizational principles that are incompatible but their existence is also based on the survival of the other lifestyles. When it comes to consumption, it is one's lifestyle that is dominant. As she writes, attacking theories of consumption based on individualist psychology, *"cultural alignment is the strongest predictor of preferences in a wide variety of fields."* (1997:23. Authors' italics).

This means, when it comes to individuals deciding on tourist destinations and other aspects of travel, it is a person's grid-group identification that is probably determinant, along with that person's desire to avoid members of other grid-group lifestyles. Thompson, Ellis and Wildavsky (1990) state this notion in a slightly different way. As they explain, (1990:57) "If preferences inhered in individuals, there would have to be a separate explanation for each individual. Social science, not to mention society, would be impossible."

Douglas concludes that shopping [includes all types of shopping ranging from food choices to clothing, housing, cars and in the present context travel] should be seen as "agonistic" in nature. She writes, "The shopper is not expecting to develop a personal identity by choice of commodities; that would be too difficult. Shopping is agonistic, a struggle to define not what one is but what one is not. When we include not one cultural bias, but four, and when we allow that each is bringing its critique against the others, and when we see that the shopper is adopting postures of cultural defiance, then it all makes sense." (1997:30)

This comment suggests a semiotic aspect to choice. Her comment is very similar to one made by Saussure (1966) in his classic text *Course in General Linguistics.* Defining concepts, he writes "Concepts are purely differential and defined not by their positive content but negatively by their relations with the other terms of the system. (1915/1966:117). He adds "The precise characteristics" of concepts "is in being what others are not."

(1915/1966:117). "In language," he writes, "there are only differences" (1915/1966:120) and the same applies to the way we differentiate ourselves from members of other grid-groups and make choices involving preferences for goods and services of all kinds, including travel and tourism.

According to grid-group theory, the choices tourists make about where to travel are profoundly shaped by what we might describe as the unconscious imperatives in their particular grid-group identification and also, to a considerable extent, by their desire to avoid being with members of other lifestyles. Grid-group theory provides us now with a new typology for tourists, to add to those by scholars who have generated their own tourism typologies.

Plog (1974) asserted that tourist preferences were based on psychological factors, in large measure the ability to tolerate risk. He suggested that tourists could be grouped into the following categories: Psychocentrics -Near Psychocentrics-Midcentrics-Near Allocentrics- Allocentrics. Cohen (1972) suggested there are four kinds of tourists: Organized Mass Tourist-Individual Mass Tourist-Explorer- Drifter. McKercher, Wong and Lau (2006) suggest in "How tourists consume a destination" that there are six kinds of tourists: Wanderers-Tour-takers-Pre-Planners-Explorers-Uncommitteds- Intimidateds.

The above indicates that tourism scholars have been imaginative and ingenious in thinking up tourism typologies, but the problem is that it is possible to classify tourists and other aggregates of people in an almost endless number of ways. All of these typologies, grid-group theory asserts, have limitations because they are based on the observations of the researchers. What grid-group theory asserts is that there is a limited number of what we call grid-group lifestyles that cover the most important human relations.

There are, grid-group theory asserts, four, and only four, kinds of tourists based on their grid-group lifestyles: Hierarchists (also termed Hierarchical Elitists); Individualists (also termed Competitive Individualists); Egalitarians (also termed Enclavists) and Fatalists (also termed Isolates).

The value of this typology is that it is based on the two fundamental problems all people face— "Who am I and what should I do?" or as Wildavsky explained, what group do I belong to, and are the boundaries weak or strong, and are there few or many rules and prescriptions to which I am subject.

Let us summarize, then. There are many different kinds of tourism experiences available to travelers, such as adventure tourism, sex tourism, disaster tourism, medical tourism, cultural tourism, etc. Many typologies for different kinds of tourists have been elaborated by scholars but there are, grid-group theory asserts, only a very limited number of grid-group lifestyles available to individuals. It is their membership in one of these four grid-group lifestyles that shapes their preferences and their consumption of everything, from mass mediated texts to food, drink and holidays. But people can change their lifestyles and thus change their preferences for kinds of touristic experiences.

The Postmodern Problematic

Grid-group theory is modernist in that it posits rational decision- making by members of each grid-group lifestyle. But postmodernism, which attacks modernist rationality and which attacks stylistic purity and fuses all kinds of opposites together, raises questions about whether grid-group theory is applicable in a postmodern world.   In one of the more celebrated explanations of postmodernism, Lyotard (1984) writes in *The Postmodern Condition* (1984:76):

> Eclecticism is the degree zero of contemporary general culture: one listens to reggae, watches a Western, eats McDonald's food for lunch and local cuisine for dinner, wears Paris perfume in Tokyo and "retro" clothes in Hong Kong: knowledge is a matter for TV games. It is easy to find a public for eclectic works. By becoming kitsch, art panders to the confusions which reigns in the "taste" of patrons.

Postmodernism suggests, then, that it is no longer possible to make the kinds of distinctions people are asked to make when thinking about their consumption preferences, which are supposed to be congruent with the dictates of their grid-group lifestyle identities. The pastiche, which mixes all kinds of things together, is a postmodern art form par excellence.

Postmodernist thinkers such as Jean Baudrillard (1998) have argued that there is now an element of compulsion in all forms of consumption, which now is seen as a duty rather than a pleasure. As he writes in *The Consumer Society: Myths and Structures* (1998:80):

> Modern man spends less and less of his life in production within work and more of it in the *production* and continual innovation of his own needs and well-being. He must constantly see to it that all of his potentialities, all his consumer capacities are mobilized. If he forgets to do so, he will be gently and insistently reminded that he has no right not to be happy… You have to try *everything,* for consumerist man is haunted by the fear of "missing" something, some form of enjoyment." Into this void, it is suggested, travel and tourism offers an ideal way to satisfy this need to exploit one's potentials for thrills and gratifications of various kinds.

Many philosophers and thinkers continue to debate what postmodernism is and isn't and whether it is still relevant. Jameson, in his book *Postmodernism or, The Cultural Logic of Late Capitalism,* argues it is really an advanced form of advanced capitalism and others have suggested that postmodernism is anything you want it to be. Some thinkers argue that postmodernism is now irrelevant since we live in a post-postmodernist world.

Conclusions

I have argued that grid-group theory provides a better understanding of consumer preferences relating to tourism and travel than other typologies. Other typologies, it can be argued, are classification systems that are arbitrary and not grounded in a theory that limits them in any way.   There are some interesting questions that relate to grid-group theory. For example, how does it explain the consumption behavior of children? One answer may be that children rapidly pick up the consumer preferences of their parents and identify with their parental grid-group identities at a relatively early age. In *The Culture Code,* Rapaille (2006) suggests that children become "coded" with national and other codes by the time they are seven and that marketers must understand these codes if they are to be able to reach their target audiences and shape their decision making. We can then posit that young children become enculturated into the grid-group lifestyle of their parents or families in the countries where they are raised.

Another problem with grid-group theory is that it recognizes that people often move from one lifestyle to another, though this is very difficult for fatalists, unless they win a lottery or chance enables them to escape from their status at the bottom of the social order. Thus, for example, individualists who lose their ability to determine their economic destinies may become egalitarians. An acquaintance of one of the authors who was a well-paid pilot and dedicated individualist found himself in a precarious economic position as a result of changes that took place in the airline for which he worked and ended up joining a labor union. In some cases, hierarchist "schismatics" break with their lifestyle to identify with egalitarian ones. There are, as Thompson, Ellis and Wildavsky (1990) point out in *Cultural Theory,* many kinds of change between lifestyles that are possible within the four lifestyles. That means it is difficult to be certain, when considering tourism, for example, which member of which lifestyles would most logically desire a certain kind of travel. The positive aspect of these changes between lifestyles is that the possibility of change and the fact that changes do occur leads to increased stability in society.

The fact that there can be movement from one lifestyle to another makes it difficult to predict consumer behavior. Are persons reading *Architectural Digest* demonstrating their affiliation with a hierarchist lifestyle or are they members of an individualist or egalitarian lifestyle contemplating identifying with a hierarchist one and adopting that lifestyle? Which kind of travel arrangements are they contemplating—one congruent with their identity as individualists or one based on their desire to identify with hierarchism and their notions about what kind of a holiday is congruent with a hierarchist lifestyle? Whatever the case, members of the four lifestyles all need one another for society to prosper. Social relations are maintained because of their ability to generate preferences, which, we can suggest, then generate and reinforce social relations.

It would be an interesting challenge for tourism researchers to see if they can find ways of testing grid-group theory as it applies to travel and tourism by creating an instrument that would enable scholars to determine the grid-group affiliations for different kinds of tourists and travelers. Grid-group theory has formal elegance but whether it can be translated into empirical research that enables scholars to test its efficacy remains a matter yet to be resolved.

REFERENCES

Baudrillard, J. 1998 The *Consumer Society*. London Sage.

Berger, A.A. (Ed.) *Political Culture and Public Opinion.* New Brunswick, NJ: Transaction Publications

Berger, A.A. *2004 Deconstructing Travel: Cultural Perspectives on Tourism*. Walnut Creek, CA: AltaMira Press.

Berger, A.A. 2005 *Media Analysis Techniques.* Thousand Oaks, CA: Sage.

Douglas, M. 1997 "In Defence of Shopping," *In The Shopping Experience*, P. Falk and C. Campbell, eds. London: Sage.

Douglas, M., and B. Isherwood 1979 *The World of Goods: Towards An Anthropology of Consumption*.   London: Routledge.

Jameson, Fredric. 1991. *Postmodernism or, The Cultural Logic of Late Capitalism.* Durham, NC: Duke University Press

Lyotard, J.-F. 1984 *The Postmodern Condition: A Report on Knowledge*. Minneapolis, MN: University of Minnesota Press.

MacCannell, D. 1976 *The Tourist: A New Theory of the Leisure Class.* New York: Schocken Books.

Rapaille, C. 2006 *The Culture Code: An Ingenious Way to Understand Why People Around the World Live and Buy as They Do*. New York: Broadway Books.

Saussure, F.De. 1966 *Course in General Linguistics*. New York: McGraw Hill.

Schwartz, B. 2004 *Paradox of Choice: Why More is Less*. New York: ECCO.

Thompson, M., Ellis R., and Wildavsky, A. 1990 *Cultural Theory.*Boulder, Colorado: Westview Press.

Wildavsky, A. 1989 "Choosing Preferences by Constructing Institutions: A Cultural Theory of Preference Formation." *American Political Science Review* 81.

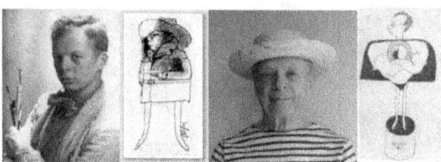

About the Author

Arthur Asa Berger is professor emeritus of Broadcast and Electronic
Communication Arts at San Francisco State University, where he taught
between 1965 and 2003. He graduated in 1954 from the University of
Massachusetts, where he majored in literature and philosophy. He received
an MA degree in journalism and creative writing from the University of
Iowa in 1956. He was inducted into the Hall of Fame of the University of
Iowa School of Journalism and Mass Communication in 2009. He was
drafted shortly after graduating from Iowa and served in the U.S. Army in
the Military District of Washington in Washington DC, where he was a
feature writer and speech writer in the District's Public Information Office.
He also wrote about high school sports for the *Washington Post* on weekend
evenings while in the army. Berger spent a year touring Europe after he got
out of the Army and then went to the University of Minnesota, where he
received a Ph.D. in American Studies in 1965. He wrote his dissertation on
the comic strip *Li'l Abner.*
          In 1963-64, he had a Fulbright to Italy and taught at the
University of Milan, where he met Umberto Eco and socialized with him
and his colleagues. He spent a year as visiting professor at the Annenberg
School for Communication at The University of Southern California in Los
Angeles in 1984 and two months in the fall of 2007 as visiting professor at
the School of Hotel and Tourism at the Hong Kong Polytechnic University.
He spent a month lecturing at Jinan University in Guangzhou and ten days
lecturing at Tsinghua University in Beijing in Spring, 2009. He spent a
month in 2012 as a Fulbright Senior Specialist in Argentina, lecturing on
semiotics and cultural criticism and three weeks lecturing on media and
communications at Teheran University in Iran in May, 2015.
          He is the author of more than one hundred and thirty articles
published in the United States and abroad, numerous book reviews, and
more than 60 books on the mass media, popular culture, humor, tourism,
Russian, Arabic, Swedish, Korean, Spanish, Turkish, Farsi, and Chinese,
and he has lectured in more than a dozen countries in the course of his
career. Berger is married, has two children and four grandchildren, and
lives in Mill Valley, California. He enjoys foreign travel and dining in
ethnic restaurants. He can be reached by e-mail at
arthurasaberger@gmail.com.

Here are some of my books published in recent years:

Ocean Travel and Cruising, 2004 (Haworth)
Deconstructing Travel: A Cultural Perspective, 2004 (AltaMira Press)
Making Sense of Media: Key Texts in Media and Cultural Studies, 2004 (Blackwell)
Shop Till You Drop. 2004. (Rowman& Littlefield)
The Kabbalah Killings. 2004. (PulpLit)
Vietnam Tourism. 2005. (Haworth)
Mistake in Identity: A Cultural Studies Murder Mystery 2005. (AltaMira)
50 Ways to Understand Communication. 2006. Rowman & Littlefield.
Thailand Tourism. 2008. (Haworth Hospitality and Tourism Press)
The Golden Triangle. 2008. (Transaction Books).
The Academic Writer's Toolkit: A User's Manual. 2008. (Left Coast Press)
What Objects Mean: An Introduction to Material Culture 2009. (Left Coast Press)
Tourism in Japan: An Ethno-Semiotic Analysis. 2010   (Channel View Publications)
The Cultural Theorist's Book of Quotations. 2010. (Left Coast Press)
The Objects of Affection: Semiotics and Consumer Culture. 2010. (Palgrave)
Understanding American Icons. 2012. (Left Coast Press).
Media, Myth and Society. 2012. (Palgrave Pivot)
Theorizing Tourism. 2012. (Left Coast Press).
Bali Tourism. 2013. (Haworth).
A Year Amongst the UK:. Marin Arts Press.
Dictionary of Advertising and Marketing Concepts. 2013 (Left Coast Press)
Messages: An Introduction to Communication. 2014   (Left Coast Press)
Gizmos. 2015 (Palgrave) in Press.

www.ingramcontent.com/pod-product-compliance
Lightning Source LLC
Chambersburg PA
CBHW060410290526
45791CB00002B/681